D1636764

GEORGE HILWAY

A

DAY

★ ★ ★ In The ★ ★ ★

WRITE

A Collection Of
One Man's Social Media Posts
From 2009-2020

A Day in The Write

©2022 George Hilway

Print ISBN: 978-1-66783-578-5

eBook ISBN: 978-1-66783-579-2

INTRODUCTION

I SUPPOSE I ALWAYS THOUGHT I would write a book someday. But like a real book – one with chapters, and these chapters would have titles. There would also be an index, maybe a dedication page, all that kinda real book stuff. But writing an entire non-fiction book, upward of 200 pages, is a lot of work and a lot of research, and let's face it, I'm kinda lazy.

I still did want to scribe a book, though. Put all the stuff in my head, pen to paper, have people read it. Then I got the idea. *What if I already wrote my book and just didn't realize it?* I thought of all the social media posts I wrote during the past decade. I could just gather them, and presto, a book. That would be easy, right? No developmental editing or indexing required, and the chapter titles could be different years. I know that my status updates, blogs, satirical writings, and general commentary — mostly on politics, the media, the world of entertainment, current events, and life in general — are brilliant. I mean, how could all those likes from my college fraternity buddies and septuagenarian aunts be wrong? *Could I be onto something?* I wondered.

Then, I got a fortune cookie that said, "You have a way with words. You should write a book." And whether it was the MSG or my silly, stupid ego, I believed it. *This clinches it*, I thought. I spent the next few months pouring over 12 years of online creativity to weed out the very best for this book and, of course, your enjoyment.

What follows is that compilation, from 2009 through 2020, complete with dates and, where appropriate, the referenced topics. My writing style mostly employs humor, sarcasm, or satire but can also be straightforward and earnest depending on the event and my mood that day. Some topics are too grave not to evoke a slightly disgruntled response. After all, we do live in crazy times.

WARNING: I'M A POLITICAL CONSERVATIVE.

This will be made abundantly clear to you in the first few posts. I know about 30 percent of you just dropped the book in horror, disgust and doused yourself in *even* more hand sanitizer. And that's OK. As Popeye said, "I yam what I yam."

Still here? Good.

If you're offended by anything written in this book, "Sorry, not sorry." And if you're not offended by anything written in this book, then "What the hell is wrong with you?"

2009

February 3, 2009 (On Dem's Tax Troubles)

I'm having my Class-C itemized deductions checked by the firm of Geithner, Daschle, and Killefer.

February 6, 2009

Kill the Spending Bill, Volume 1

Well, folks, I just wrapped up a stint as a PA on season one of *The Real Housewives of Wausau*, so I'm a little cranky and bored. Albeit I was better treated than my last gig as the lighting dude for that Christian Bale flick. Marry that with the fact that I was hopped-up on Acme diet green tea, and I decided to copiously go over the proposed spending, I mean stimulus bill. It's with great sadness that I report that I have not been this ill since I watched the Danny DeVito and Rhea Perlman sex tape, which coincidentally contained just as much pork.

First off, some $400 million is going toward STD prevention and education. For God's sake, can't someone just grab Samantha Ronson's underwear? Not to mention money for fresh sod for the National Mall, apparently due to huge divots left by a grazing Aretha Franklin during the Inauguration. Best of all, they need $850 million for Amtrak. Folks, I rode Amtrak once, once. I screamed the whole way like a four-year-old girl being babysat by Randy Quaid. Then there's the $6 billion they need to turn federal buildings "green."

"Sit down, Michael Phelps. That's not what we mean here."

If the true intent of this proposed bill is to stimulate growth and create jobs, both of which are sorely needed now, then it fails miserably. On paper, the bill amounts to roughly $1.2 trillion, including interest, the most significant transfer of wealth to the US government since Tim Geithner paid back his taxes. Americans are hurting now. We need more tax cuts in the bill, less wasteful spending, and a new wardrobe for Michelle Obama. I hope she wasn't proud of her country when she picked out that green number. Disguising this bill as a stimulus package, instead of pork barrel spending wrapped around European-style Socialism, doesn't fool me, and it shouldn't fool you either. President Barack "BO" Obama needs to take a page from Ronald Reagan's playbook.

Gotta go now. I have to text "1" on my Verizon mobile to have Kathy Griffin blown up by an IED on *Waterboarding with the Stars*.

February 13, 2009

I Met My Idol, Dane Cook

People who know me know two things: (1) If I'm ever found unresponsive, they should immediately phone Mary-Kate Olsen, and (2) I love Dane Cook.

So, you can imagine my delight when I met Dane "Cookster" Cook, after his show in New Jersey last Super Bowl Sunday. Cook-a-lisimo could not have been any nicer.

Despite being tired from having just finished his set — two hours of ninja kicks and no punchlines will do that, Cookster was trenchantly taking notes from Louis C.K.'s book, *My Set Lists from the 1990s.* Not sure what that was all about. Anyhoo I was fueled by a cosmic combination of Pimp C's syrup and Rascal Comedy Club's fiery Paul Rodriguez wings, so I approached the talent-drained comic.

"Hi, Mr. Cook. Great set. Can I buy you a drink?" I asked.

"I don't drink. It makes me funny and ruins the integrity of my work," the star of *Waiting* and *Employee of The Month* replied.

I choked back a chuckle. *Man, is this guy never not on?*

Just then, "I am Legend's" cell phone rang. He turned away to take the call, but I could still make out demands of back-end points for *Good Luck Chuck Part Two* and inquiries about Jimmy Fallon's hairstylist. *Oops, did I just spoil some page six Hollywood gossip?* I wondered. Take it as a tip from your little *ET* insider. When Cookarama hung up, Mr. Jay Davis approached him and dutifully proclaimed that he had picked out all the brown M&M's.

Could it be? I thought. *Am I in the presence of one-half of Tourgasm?* These guys are like the Fab Four of stand-up. Only, unlike the Beatles, these lads have talent. Put that in your pipe and smoke it, Mr. Brian Epstein.

Apparently, Cookarama now does prop comedy. I damn near soiled myself laughing when a strategically placed audience member approached him, broke a Heineken bottle over his head, and screamed, "I want a friggin' refund!"

Does this guy ever stop working? I haven't seen someone go to this great depth of physical comedy for a laugh since Fatty Arbuckle murdered that whore in Cali.

Blood streamed down Cookarama's head. I suppose he had some blood packets left over from *Mr. Brooks.* It got all over his retro tight t-shirt with little stars and his ripped gray designer jeans. *Hey, did he steal that outfit from Bill Maher's wardrobe set from his HBO special, The Decider? Or did Maher borrow it from the Cook-man himself? Hmmm, which came first, the chicken or the egg?* By now, Jay Davis had smeared Cook's blood all over his clothes à la Rev. Jesse Jackson in Memphis on April 4, 1968. He tried to lead Cookie-Monster (his nickname for Dane) away when a waitress came out of nowhere and kicked Cookarama in the balls. *Can you say, workaholic?* I thought. *This guy is the consummate professional.* Apparently, a 10-cent tip on two Pellegrino's and a Zima isn't a lot of money in Montclair, NJ. I suppose the Liberal media is correct; physical violence is more prevalent on Super Bowl Sunday than any other day of the year.

Cookster stumbled on the Tourgasm bus, which Dr. Gulman and Dr. Kelly had hastily transformed into a makeshift mobile hospital.

"Oh, what a vicious circle we've gotten ourselves into." He yelled in a dazed state before passing out in their arms.

They sped away for their next stop in comedy heaven, and I couldn't help but wonder if I would ever again witness such talent. I looked up and caught the opening scene of an *According to Jim* rerun on the bar's corner T. V. Things are looking up. *Only in New Jersey, kids, only in New Jersey!*

February 22, 2009

Oscar Picks

Not sure if this year's Oscar Awards Ceremony will receive the same Nielsen audience as in the past. For one thing, Jack Nicholson will not be attending. Apparently, Larry David's line that only blind people and assholes wear sunglasses indoors finally got to him. Hugh Jackman is the host, and word is the presenters kept confidential until now are a family of chimps. On that note, I'm going to miss Travis terribly. This week's outburst was his worst since he complained about Morgan Fairchild's acting while filming those Old Navy ads in the late '90s.

Also, it appears the recession is hitting Tinseltown. Rumor has it those once swanky, swab grab bags for presenters valued at over $70,000 are down to a few dollar-store coupons and an Abreva pump spray. Despite this, I felt it was a pretty good year for cinema. So good that it compelled me to see a few of the nominations.

With movies, where you see them is almost as important as what you see. The surroundings, city, and audience demographic all play a big part in augmenting your enjoyment of the flick. I first discovered this magic of movie milieu at a midnight double feature screening of *Pooty Tang* and *Juwanna Man* at the Magic Johnson Theaters in Inglewood. So, without further ado, here we go.

Frost/Nixon

I saw this Ron Howard vehicle with my good buddy, Ohio Rep. Dennis Kucinich, at an independent theater in Berkley. Although I think Hollywood took some liberties with the script. Did Nixon really have horns and a tail? Did the 37th President swallow a makeup artist because he couldn't reduce his on-camera five o'clock shadow? Despite extensive Wikipedia research, I could not substantiate this incident.

The progressive northern Cali audience, though, ate it up. And they came dressed up just like those acned virgin nerds do for a *Star Wars* flick. Only this time, they had pitchforks, torches, nooses, and signs that read, "honk for impeachment and beheading." Halfway through the movie, I nudged Denny and asked if he liked it or not. He mumbled something about having to close Gitmo sooner than BO ordered and went back to his vegan hot dog. Man, that guy has a one-track mind.

Overall, I give *Frost/Nixon* an A. The acting was superb. Frank Langella gave the performance of a lifetime (gotta support my fellow Garden Staters). He did an intimate character portrayal instead of a great impression, tempting with historical figures. This movie gets my vote as Best Picture.

Milk

In keeping with my better judgment, I turned down Michael Musto's offer to watch the film with him at a theater in Chelsea. I could just picture it, a devilishly winking Musto repeatedly asking if I want my popcorn buttered. Instead, I saw the flick with a cousin who's obviously struggling with his sexual identity. When I asked him what he thought, he said, "I think James Franco is cute, ugh, I mean, the mise-en-scène was great."

Gus Van Sant does a fantastic job of inter-weaving archival footage at proper times during the film. Sean Penn, predictably, does a good job of portraying a homosexual. The writing is good, and Franco adds some grade A depth. Although Van Sant won't win Best Director, that will likely go to whoever directed Tyler Perry's *Madea Goes to Jail*; he still directed a wonderful film.

Slumdog Millionaire

I saw a bootleg copy of this at a convenience store with slushie ice and a scratch-off lotto ticket. The hip, stylistic Bollywood invasion continues. Look for this one to take home Best Director for Danny Boyle.

The Wrestler

Mickey Rourke is back, McMahon! Sorry, I'm still reeling from watching this at the AMC theater in Asbury Park, where I was hit with a folding chair upon entering and sat on a syringe strategically placed on all the seats by a crazed usher who insisted I call him the Ram. Seriously, Rourke is amazing, and he smartly utilizes this script as a recipe for comeback success. I guess life imitates art. Mickey wins Best Actor, and I'm looking forward to his acceptance speech the same way Chris Brown looks forward to advance copies of *The Ike Turner Story*.

Best Actress Award

As for the Best Actress category, I doubt I'll be seeing *Rachel Getting Married*, and it'll be a *Frozen River* in hell before I see *The Reader*, and if I happen to see it on cable one day, I will be a- *Changeling* the channel.

Best Supporting Actor

For Best Supporting actor, I gave it to Heath Ledger the minute Mary-Kate Olsen's cell phone rang. Nice to see Downey Jr. get nominated, especially for a comedy. But if a White man portraying a White man who's portraying a Black man was a requisite for an Oscar, then Wayne Brady's mantel would be full.

Hope ya'll enjoy the show!

March 1, 2009

I'm now friends with Yoko Ono via the People You May Loathe tool.

March 22, 2009

BO's March Madness

There have been worse weeks for leaders: Custer at Little Big Horn, a psychotic anti-Semite, stuck with a struggling B-movie German actress in a bunker, and the time when Mary Todd Lincoln petulantly nagged her husband to finally take her to see a show. But despite the AIG bonus catastrophe, calls for Treasury Secretary Tim "Turbo Tax" Geithner to step down, and worries about the increasing amount of toxic assets on the balance sheets of the nation's banks, BO has taken the opportunity to do what we expect from all great leaders when the going gets tough, the tough get going to California.

To quell the fears of anxious Americans, BO took to where he feels most comfortable, the campaign trail. Still suffering from the whiplash caused by the second teleprompter he installed in his White House bedroom so he can reach verbal sexual climax with the Frost Lady without stammering, a neck-braced BO addressed a packed town hall in Orange County,

"Do you like the brace? It's Teddy's from the Kopechne funeral."

As hundreds of guilt-ridden White Liberals fainted, BO got down to business.

"I know many of you are scared. You're uncertain about the future. You have legitimate concerns about rising tuition costs and the healthcare crisis facing America. Some of you have recently lost a job or know someone who did. Some of you are wondering if your job is safe. But I want to assure every one of you that I have filled out my brackets, and with Allah's help, my Tar Heels are going all the way, baby."

Dragging off a Kool, he continued, "Some people think my recovery plan won't work. I know there are naysayers out there, and let me just address them by saying, 'Coach K, you shouldn't be worried about me worrying about the economy. You need to worry about whether Duke's man-to-man defense can stop Tyler Hansbrough.' America, you need to understand that my cabinet and I are on top of it. We have been in close contact with Greg Gumbel and Seth Davis. This week, through my live-look-ins from the war room, I will closely monitor the situation in all first-round action from Philadelphia to Boise, and that's a promise."

The 44th President then exited the stage to thundering applause and shouts of "Yes, We Can" from the MSNBC crew.

Then it was on to the Valley and Burbank, where BO made history as he became the first sitting president to appear on *The Tonight Show*. He used the occasion to address a specific demographic group, which, he felt, for too long had not been publicly attacked by a leader of the Free World: the physically and mentally challenged. Due to his Special Olympics gaffe, which later turned out to be a pre-show recommendation from Vice President Biden to "win the crowd over," BO had to issue a public apology.

"I, in no way, meant to demean or make fun of the mentally challenged, many of whom, might I add, voted for me in November. Whether you are intellectually disabled, mentally handicapped, or Tony Danza, you are all special people, and no matter how 'Honky' I find bowling to be, you are all heroes in the game of life."

Later that day, back in Washington, BO canceled a meeting with the Fed chairman to help Michele in the garden. "Bernanke can wait; the arugulas can't."

April 9, 2009

I can't wait for the day when Facebook acquiesces to Sharia Law.

April 28, 2009

Will the Real BO Please Drink Up?

At last week's "Hump Night" bash at the White House, an unidentified guest "Andrew Luster-ed" a drink he mistakenly believed belonged to "Eight Ball" Ashley Biden. The unintended recipient, BO, drank the narcotics-laced glass heartily and immediately after that felt the truth serum effects kick in. Behaving like a WWII POW heavy under the spell of MDMA, BO launched into an unscripted, un(tele)prompted diatribe which gave those present, and now all of you here in cyberspace, a glimpse into our commander-in-grief's beliefs.

Above the din of glasses, a sweaty BO stood up to toast. "Here's to the rise of insurgency in Iraq. America, God, I love this place. Where else on earth can someone as indefensible as me be elected to lead? I'm constituted of such loose, moral fabric that the slightest tug from a once-proud Republican opposition can undress me, baring once and for all that the emperor has no clothes.

Where do I start? First, a shout-out to my friends in the mainstream media. You know who you are. Without your one-sided, biased reporting and unabashed campaign support, the American people might have gotten to know the real me.

The Liberal media is so in love with me that they will utter embarrassing statements like "I have this thrill running up my leg." With impartiality out of the way, everyone was on board to get a man of color elected president. I am not particularly adept at thinking on my feet, hence the teleprompters and the news conferences that have a *West Wing* episode feel, rather than anything, say, unscripted. Only a few reporters will be allowed follow-up questions, those whose style is more *Taxicab Confessions* than hard news. Safe to say, Helen Thomas will once again have the same front row seat in the briefing room she's enjoyed since the Chester A. Arthur administration in 1881.

Because of my associations with 60's radicals like Bill Ayers and his wife Bernardine Dohrn, I wouldn't have been able to receive a security clearance to mop up excrement from the Hoover Building. However, I was allowed to become the 6th star General of the US Army, head of the executive branch of the US government, and leader of the free world. God, I love this place!

Only in America can you open your political career in the living room of those who bombed the US Capitol building and police stations in NYC and still be elected president. Truth is stranger than fiction. God, I love America. I mean, the former territory of North Mexico. I even convinced the foolish American people that even though I spent 20 years in a church led by Reverend Jeremiah Wright, I didn't hear any of his persistent, anti-American rhetoric. At best, I'm naive and hard-of-hearing. At worst, I'm enthusiastically nodding my head during his hate sermons.

Thanks to my Jewish friends, by far, my largest financial backers during the 2008 campaign, despite my close ties to Rashid Khalini. One can only wonder about the mental disconnect between American Jews and their relatives in Israel. Israel, whose position in the Middle East is tenuous at best, can no longer rely on their family and friends of the same faith back here in the States for support. American Jews backed a man for president who supports a world that welcomes Israeli haters like Khalidi and their twisted ideologies. Speaking of Israel, kudos to my friend and Holocaust denier, Iranian President Mahmoud Ahmadinejad. I welcome talks with him and members of his state without pre-conditions even though Iran is listed as a state sponsor of terror and has nuclear ambitions.

But let me make this clear, this administration will not deal with or speak to Conservative radio talk show hosts. Can you hear me, Hannity? Henceforth known as the Obama Doctrine, we will not differentiate between those who broadcast Conservative opinions and those that listen to them. We will pursue radio stations that provide airtime or haven to Conservatism. Every radio station in every region now has a decision to make, you're either with the Conservatives or with us. From this day forward, any radio station that continues to harbor or support Conservatism will be regarded by the United States as a hostile regime.

Thanks to Senators Debbie Stabenow of Michigan and Jeff Bingamon of New Mexico, who have renewed the interest in the Fairness Doctrine, the days when Conservative voices have an edge in any form of media are coming to an end. Will the Fairness Doctrine apply to other mass media sources, PBS, print journalism, and major television broadcasting networks? Not if they continue to be dominated by Liberals and Liberal ideals.

I will let the American people believe that my wife's statement that this is the first time in her adult life that she is proud of her country was a mistake because she was just talking off the top of her head even though she read it off prepared statements in two speeches in Milwaukee and Madison, Wisconsin. I'll position Michelle as a victim. She'll insinuate, some might even say threaten, that America is a downright mean country. She'll play the victim card until blue in the face even though she had a privileged upbringing, attended an Ivy League school, and her brother is the head coach of one of the top college basketball programs in the nation, all while "talking like a White girl."

As for my cabinet, although we will continuously vote to raise your taxes, we won't pay our own. Don't believe me? Just look at my laughable nominations to key cabinet positions. Daschle, Killefer, Geithner, Sebelius, etc. Speaking of cabinet positions, even though I'm staring 100 days in the Oval Office right in the face, I still haven't filled most spots. America's Health and Human Services top spot is incredulously still open, even though we're facing a possible pandemic breakout of the Swine Flu.

As for discarding terms like the "war on terror," if we don't use a phrase like that, we are less likely to be attacked (not really). As we all know, nothing draws the murderous ire of Islamic fundamentalist terrorists like the vernacular we use. Sure, I'll release CIA interrogation memos that endanger us and further enrage and educate terrorists looking to harm us; and will label

American military personnel who return home as Right-wing extremists and possible threats to homeland security.

When I'm representing America overseas, Tokyo Rose has nothing on me. I'll bow to Mid-East despots, awkwardly hug a Queen, give her a gaudy I-Pod, commiserate with Hugo, join his book club, and sit quietly through Daniel Ortega's One-Night Stand. As for giving aid and comfort to the enemy overseas, damn right. America has been arrogant, and its days as a global superpower are done. I'll glasnost up to people like Fidel and Raoul, who have slaughtered scores of citizens who spoke up against their regime but will not rule out trials for Bush administration officials. Although America does not torture, I'm happy to offer a limp-wristed hand to leaders of nations that do. My skin color makes me an ideal vehicle for the American Far-left to promulgate their radical agenda while insulating me from legitimate critiques. Because as you see, any criticism of my policies, beliefs, or life values, is just racism. The massive numbers of Americans organizing Tea Parties on April 15 were just dressed up, tea-bagging bigots. Anyway, I guess I'm supposed to say I was unaware they were organizing in the first place.

As for my massive spending bill, a gargantuan $787 billion of your money ($1.1 trillion with interest) is a Trojan Horse hiding Socialism. It will bankrupt the government for generations to come and leave a massive debt for your children, grandchildren, and great-grandchildren all while doing nothing to inject life into the economy. Instead, it will lead to super inflation and turn unemployment lines into breadlines.

My chief of staff, Rahm Emanuel, famously said, "you never want a serious crisis to go to waste." This economic stimulus package represents the largest transfer of wealth and power to the government. When the government has power over the people, it does not give it back to the people, even though we are a government of the people, by the people, for the people. I believe the government has the right to take from the people and seize the wealth of those willing to work for it, like Joe the Plumber. For too long, those that have worked hard, provided, and have been the single greatest creator of job growth through small business enterprises have prospered. To these people, I say, the days of American prosperity vis-à-vis the free market are over.

Jim Cramer and Rick Santelli got it right; I am the single greatest destroyer of wealth in American history. Just because you have worked hard and think that you should keep, re-invest, or create jobs through the fruits of your labor is an antiquated notion. Think of the spending bill as a pre-cursor to the government soon taking your money and spending it on massive pork projects, earmarks, and production of a cradle-to-grave welfare state. All while you, the American citizen, have zero input in these matters. Instead, I intend to turn over complete control to a massive, bloated bureaucracy all while raising your taxes. And, on the rare occasion, some member of the press has the temerity to ask me about out-of-control government spending, I will childishly say, "Well, Bush started it."

Occasionally, I will speak my mind, most likely in private or when I think I'm not being taped. Hence, my bitter, angry Americans clinging to their guns and religious comment. Sometimes, I will say crazy things on T.V. and give everyone a glimpse of my sick, twisted sense of humor, like when that Tim Russert-come-lately, Jay Leno, made me exhale a joke about The Special Olympics. I intend to nationalize healthcare even though I know it will sharply raise our nation's cancer mortality rate because some medications and operations will not be allowed. National healthcare has not worked any-where-including here in the US, where states like Tennessee have previously had it. Doctors will be squeezed, breakthroughs in medicine will be stilted because, without free market competition, there is no incentive to create a superior alternative product. To the 9 percent of ovarian cancer patients who would have otherwise survived had I not intervened, surely your lives are a small price to pay in support of nationalizing Mother America.

How far will some go to get to know me? I have been asked to be the commencement ceremony speaker at The University of Notre Dame. Honestly, when Michelle and I first heard about the invitation, we were roll-ing on the ground laughing so hard you'd have thought we were watching a

Robert Gibbs press conference. Only in America folks can a pro-choice zealot like me be asked to give the commencement address at the holiest of holy Catholic institutions in the world. And folks, I'm super pro-choice, not just the casual way Planned Parenthood goes about it. Oh no, I've taken it one step further and voted yes on a bill in the Illinois Senate to kill a baby born alive after a botched abortion. Some call this a late, late, third-term abortion. State and Federal law enforcement have another name for it, first-degree murder. Oh, wait. wait. What have I been saying? I'm feeling faint. I mean, nappy time."

May 13, 2009

How Waterboarding Washes with BO, You Can't Do That on Teleprompter

At his latest primetime press conference (kudos to the Fox Network, by the way, for not airing it), BO declared that he believes waterboarding is torture. Yes, that's right. Until about four years ago, waterboarding was something I thought was an event in the X games that is now deemed torture. Waterboarding essentially amounts to the same treatment the losing families endured on Super Sloppy Double Dare. No word yet if the BO administration is considering a war crimes trial for Marc Summers or a possible governmental asset seizure of the Pie-Pod.

BO's problem with the method of waterboarding as an interrogation tool is that the terror detainees had water splashed in their face, although they had not uttered trigger phrases such as "wet" or "water." BO went on to say that type of interrogation technique would only be tolerated if utilized as an introduction to the opposite sketches or, at the very least, if "that motor-mouth Lisa Ruddy has it coming." Christine "Moose" McGlade, Ross Ewich and Kevin Kubusheskie were unavailable for comment.

One can argue that waterboarding was successfully used on 9/11 mastermind Khalid Sheik Mohammed to gain information and prevent future attacks. However, it's not clear if the method worked due to his fear of drowning or just his fear of coming into contact with water. Judging by Mohammed's midcareer headshots, I'm assuming the latter. Some will say that if you torture a man long enough, he will concoct any story, tell the torturer anything he wants to hear, just to have it stop. Still, I'll take my chances. An ounce of prevention is worth a pound of cure.

Before BO banned waterboarding, whether it would continue to be used as an interrogation technique was irrelevant. The mere fact that this debate was publicized educated Al-Qaeda and other terrorist groups on what to expect and how to deal with it, thereby rendering waterboarding impotent. I find it troubling that our current administration wants to declassify every document that details the CIA's treatment of detainees at Guantanamo Bay but wants the Census Bureau to report directly to the White House.

At that same press conference, BO said he recently read a piece (which remained un-cited) in which he learned that Winston Churchill didn't torture Germans during WWII. Really? Does BO believe that despite all the evidence to the contrary? The British starved and brutally beat German captures, induced drug stupors, threatened hangings, and forced them to sleep naked in cold tubs. At the same time, the British themselves were tortured in unspeakable ways in concentration camps; some were even plied with something called toothpaste. As a side note, I've compiled a list of other things BO believes:

- Lee Harvey Oswald acted alone.
- ACORN is a legitimate organization with stringent voter-registration policies.
- If you swallow apple seeds, an apple tree will grow in your stomach.
- Santa Claus, Bigfoot, and The Loch Ness Monster not only exist but have also failed to pay their back taxes, making them ideal candidates for his cabinet.

The Far-left is famous for moral equivalency in international matters. CNN gives equal time and outrage to Israeli missiles taking out Hamas terrorists as it does to Palestinians blowing up a pizza shop in the Gaza and killing teenage girls listening to The Jonas Brothers on their I-Pod despite the obvious fact that one is a pre-emptive strike on terrorists and the other is the intentional killing of innocent civilians. Liberals here in the States are quick to display anger at the idea of waterboarding being used at all against detainees at Gitmo. So, why is it that the loony Left doesn't exhibit outrage when Iraqi insurgents blow up American contractors and then drag and hang their charred remains from a bridge in Fallujah? These stories are usually relegated to page A-19 of *The New York Times* next to a piece about how Governor David Patterson is upset because he answered the iron again and someone rearranged his furniture. Could it be that there is a double standard being applied? The hell, you say. Suppose the Lefties really think that America is a superior nation with higher standards of morality and ethics than, say, those from the Middle East. How does that wash with their time-honored mantra of the dangers of espousing ethnocentrism? I thought that in the context of their utopian world view, all nations and people would melt into one loose moral code of behavior and culture (that is, unless you want to continue speaking Spanish once illegally entering into the United States) vis-à-vis a secularized cradle-to-grave welfare state.

While we're at it, why does a preponderance of the Left want Geneva Convention standards applied to captured terrorists even though they do not wear uniforms or fly a flag? It seems convenient that the loonies can point to a strict reading of the Army's manual not allowing torture or waterboarding while bending and distorting the Geneva Convention rules to protect captured terrorists who want to harm America.

These days, the moveon.org-ers and George Soros crowd demonstrate an "America last" attitude in most matters. No foreign country, terrorist group, or rogue nation can destroy America. Our real enemy lives at home, inside our borders, among us. Only time will tell if traditional Americans have the gumption, strength, integrity, and moral fortitude to combat them.

May 28, 2009 (On Sonia Sotomayor's Nomination to the Supreme Court)

If higher authorities overturned 60 percent of my decisions at work, I would be out of a job. But then again, I'm a White male who often comes to worse conclusions than some extra on *El Gordo y La Flaca*.

May 28, 2009

I think it's great that La Raza will soon have a voice on the Supreme Court. Well, I guess it's time for me to re-patriate the ol' country.

May 28, 2009

I think Frank Luntz should conduct a polling response about his toupee.

June 10, 2009

This year only, head on down to crazy Barack's for "Cash For Clunkers." I won't be beat!

June 25, 2009 (On Michael Jackson's Death)

NAMBLA's flags are at half-staff.

July 3, 2009

More Americans "strongly disapprove" of BO's job performance than "strongly approve." Now I've got a thrill running up MY leg.

August 12, 2009 (On Obama's Speech)

"FedEx and UPS are doing just fine. It's the Post Office that's always having problems," said President Barack Obama. Thanks for proving our point, genius.

September 30, 2009

Looking out my window, I see that the empire state building is lit red and yellow to celebrate communist China's 60th anniversary. Wtf! Did I miss a memo? I guess Manhattan Libs think that 60 years of human rights abuses and unrivaled mass pollution deserve a tribute.

October 3, 2009 (On Chicago Losing the Olympics)

How dare the IOC not be impressed that Madam Michelle's father had multiple sclerosis? Pure and blatant racism that Chicago was not chosen! Please join Kanye, the good Reverends Jesse, Al, and I in boycotting Rio.

November 3, 2009

Strange Days

"Nobody told me there'd be days like these." That musical line, the hook in a 1984 posthumous hit for John Lennon, is very apt for the present. Recently we've learned that it's perfectly fine to falsely ascribe synthetically manufactured racially divisive quotes to a Conservative radio talk show host to keep him from becoming a minority owner of an NFL team. At the same time, it is not ok to denounce racial epithets actually said by a rapper/Liberal/minority who is part-owner of the New Jersey Nets. The Chamber of Commerce, health insurance providers, Tea Party protestors, The Fox News Channel, and the nation of Israel are all enemies of BO's administration. But corrupt, tyrannical election-rigging terrorist leaders of Iran are not. A government that can't even effectively distribute H1N1 vaccine shots in a timely manner thinks it will be able to handle the overhaul of America's health care system and one-sixth of the nation's economy. While the head of the House of Representative's tax-writing committee who hasn't properly disclosed half-a-million dollars in cash assets, tens-of-thousands of dollars in investment income, and his ownership of two pieces of property in New Jersey thus far gets to keep his chairmanship, a congressman who accurately points out falsehoods in the president's healthcare speech has to apologize. Liberals believe that a beer tax will ultimately lower gonorrhea rates, and a soda tax will ultimately lower obesity rates, but income tax cuts will not lead to economic stimulus.

We have a commander-in-chief who has no problem flying to Denmark to personally lobby the IOC to grant his hometown the Olympic Games but has never visited our 60,000 brave troops in Afghanistan nor given the Commanding General there the requested reinforcements. The Far-left will petition to release a movie director who drugged and sodomized a 13-year-old girl but push for trials of the Bush administration members who interrogated Islamic terrorists and prevented future attacks on America. Ads targeting a New Jersey Governor's poor record of job losses, tax hikes, and property tax rebates rescues are all part of a smear campaign, while commercials making fun of his GOP challenger's weight are fair game. Strange days, indeed.

November 7, 2009 (On US House Passing Health Care Reform Bill)

Wake up, America; 220 members of Congress just declared war on your liberties.

November 26, 2009

I'm going RINO hunting real soon.

December 4, 2009

"The best way to get people out of poverty is to have them be uncomfortable in it." —Benjamin Franklin

December 15, 2009

So, how's that "Hope and Change" working' for ya, America?

December 29, 2009 (On Sen. Max Baucus' Seemingly Drunk Senate Floor Speech)

Sen. Max "Boozehound" Baucus, I haven't been that drunk since college.

December 29, 2009

Max Baucus just projectile vomited all over Barbara Boxer-film at 11:00 p.m.

December 30, 2009 (On Rush Limbaugh's Hawaii Illness)

Come on, Rush. We are pulling and praying for you.

2010

January 5, 2010 (On Insane No-Fly Lists)

So, Joan Rivers was too dangerous to fly, but not Umar Farouk Abdulmutallab? Good job, people.

January 6, 2010

Poll time, folks. Would you rather have your crotch blown up or Janet Napolitano's hairdo?

January 10, 2010

Here's how Harry Reid and Bill Clinton just called the win on CBS: "Hooray for the light-skinned Baltimore Ravens who handed the Pats their first home playoff loss since 1978. and that's no Negro dialect. Wow, '78, back when players like that were getting coffee for us. Back to you in New York."

January 11, 2010

Is Blago blacker than BO? You decide America.

January 19, 2010 (On Scott Brown Winning Sen. Ted Kennedy's Old Seat)

PMSNBC has live update tallies, whereas Fox is slow. So, I'm on MSLSD, that's fine. The look on Keith Overbite's face when Brown wins will be priceless.

Mary Jo Kopechne-Caldwell College Alum, tonight's for you, babe.

January 21, 2010

Brown victorious, Air America signs off for the last time, and the Supreme Court rules that non-media entities should also be afforded full First Amendment protections. What a week. There will be a non-alcoholic toast at my condo at 9 p.m. tonight. If you're in the area, please stop by.

January 27, 2010 (State of the Union "SOTU" Updates)

SOTU Update: Janet Napolitano will attend after recently discovering how to DVR *Cagney & Lacey.*

SOTU Update: The Salahi's have just made a fashionable late entrance.

(On Having to Unfortunately Stare at VP Biden for the SOTO)

I'm blind after spending 40 minutes staring at bad hair plugs and micro-derm-abrasion gone bad. It's like a print ad for a reverse mortgage.

SOTU Update: BO Proposes freezing Madam Pelosi's face for three more years.

SOTU Update: Mr. President, if and when the teleprompter goes down, blame Bush.

SOTU Update: After 50 minutes of blaming everything on the Bush administration policies, BO is suddenly not "interested in re-litigating the past."

SOTU Update: Yeah, how's about another tight shot of Sen. Grassley's cold sore. Huh? Who's the director of photography here, David Cronenberg?

February 5, 2010

Only a few months ago, each tenth of a percentage point in the nation's unemployment number accounted for over 200,000 jobs. Now we have continuing job losses for the month at 20,000. That equates to a 0.3 percent decline in unemployment. Believing the job numbers doesn't require a Hollywood-inspired Larry Cohen-like suspension of disbelief; it requires suspension of brain activity.

February 18, 2010 (On Dalai Lama's Visit to Washington DC)

Hey Dalai, if you insist on expressing your right to "bear arms," how about doing some push-ups and tightening up a bit?

February 20, 2010

I wonder what exactly happens in sex rehab.

February 23, 2010 (On Greece's Financial Debacle)

I just purchased the Parthenon for four dollars.

February 25, 2010 (On Sea World Animal Trainer's Death)

Orca-Gate —what did SeaWorld know, and when did they know it?

February 27, 2010 (On Attending a Game of the Woeful New Jersey Nets)

My fear of running out onto the court during a Nets game is not the threat of arrest and prosecution but rather that Vandeweghe would want me to stay in the game.

March 22, 2010 (On the Passing of Obamacare)

Nationalized healthcare in America? How can the Chinese afford this?

April 16, 2010 (On My Least Favorite Yankee Announcers)

Please sign my petition to have John Sterling, and Suzyn Waldman executed.

April 18, 2010 (Reflecting on C-Webb's NBA Career)

Based on his earnings and career numbers, Chris Webber earned $10,000 for every point he scored in the NBA. He was paid this exorbitant amount despite never leading any team he played on past the Conference Finals. Is he the most overpaid NBA player of all time?

April 28, 2010

Will everyone stop comparing Obama to Hitler? They are not alike. For one thing, Hitler didn't need a teleprompter.

May 19, 2010 (On Derek Jeter's Car Commercial)

Are we really supposed to believe that Derek Jeter drives a Ford Edge?

June 2, 2010 (On Joyce's Blown Call in the Ninth Inning Ruining Gallaraga's Perfect Game)

Yes, Jim Joyce, there have been too many perfect games in MLB already this season.

June 6, 2010 (On NBA Finals)

Did a quick shot of Dane Cook just ruin Ray Allen's performance for everyone else like it did for me? Thanks, ABC.

June 9, 2010 (On Alvin Greene's Path to Democratic Nomination in SC for Senate)

To all the unemployed Army vets who have been arrested on felony charges for showing obscene photos to college students and who win Democratic Senate primaries without campaigning or donation money, yesterday was for you.

June 15, 2010

World Traveler Trivia Question: "What's the proper way to ask how to get to the local hospital when visiting Washington DC?"

Answer: "Excuse me, Rep. Etheridge, do you support the Obama agenda?"

June 25, 2010 (On the One Year Anniversary of MJ's Death)

OK, I know it's one year to the day and all, but how many friggin' times can they play "Man in The Mirror?"

July 8, 2010 (On "The Decision")

Did Jim Gray just ask LeBron James if he was ready to admit that Pete Rose bet on baseball games he managed?

July 14, 2010

Lord, on Sunday of this week, you took away my favorite announcer, Bob Sheppard. Then on Tuesday, you took away my favorite owner, George Steinbrenner. Just so you know, Joe Girardi is my favorite manager.

August 4, 2010

That whenever any form of government becomes destructive of these ends, it is the Right of the People to alter or to abolish it, and to institute new government, laying its foundation on such principles and organizing its powers in such form … but when a long train of abuses and usurpations, it is their right, it is their duty, to throw off such government, and to provide new Guards for their future security. (Declaration of Independence)

August 21, 2010

I find it amusing that the people leading the push for Sharia Law in some fashion in this nation are the ones that would be executed first under it.

November 2, 2010 (On the GOP Taking Back the House)

The House is ours.

December 8, 2010

We'll always remember John Winston Lennon. 1940-1980.

December 13, 2010

Healthcare individual mandate ruled unconstitutional. Stay focused, America, as the fight is just beginning.

2011

January 8, 2011 (On the Shooting of US Rep. Giffords and Others in AZ)

Prayers for Rep. Giffords.

January 25, 2011 (SOTU)

SOTU Update: If both teleprompters go down, look for BO to do his impression of *The King's Speech*.

SOTU Update: Speaker Boehner is already tearing up.

SOTU Update: Tonight's speech was brought to you by China. "China, come for our human rights violations. Stay for our anti-freeze in children's toothpaste."

SOTU Update: Clean energy sources? You mean like carbon dating Helen Thomas and using her rings for fuel?

SOTU Update: All that money spent on education, and I'm happy to report that more than half of our public school teachers can now read.

SOTU Update: BO lecturing us on debt? Hmm, kinda' like Charlie Sheen teaching us how to treat a lady on a first date.

SOTU Update: Did he just call for tort reform? Somewhere in the galley, Chuck Schumer is being restrained.

SOTU Update: Simplify the tax code, so even Tim Geithner's accountant gets it.

SOTU Update: In Pakistan, Al-Qaeda is under more pressure than Jerrold Nadler's kneecaps.

SOTU Update: Free voting in Afghanistan — hopefully, the Black Panthers will allow that in south Philly one day.

SOTU Update: Get the Kleenex out; it's Boehner time!

SOTU Update: Being left-handed is a sign of improper potty training as a kid.

SOTU Update: America patiently awaits Jim Belushi's response to SOTU.

January 28, 2011 (On the Arab Spring Uprising)

I guess I picked the wrong week to bring the kids to Egypt.

February 2, 2011

Arguments of America as an intellectually superior nation are mitigated by the fact that we look to a rodent to prognosticate an early spring season or not.

February 4, 2011 (On Yankee Great's Retirement)

We'll miss you, Andy Pettitte.

February 11, 2011

Today's fun factoid — In Vermont, it is illegal for women to wear false teeth without their husband's written permission.

February 18, 2011

The only difference between Charles Manson and Keith Olbermann is that Manson had followers.

March 24, 2011

"Whether you think you can or you can't, you're right." —Henry Ford

March 24, 2011

Watching Badger game, missing Madison. Thanks, Madtown, for providing a lesson not found in any textbook. It's what they don't teach you in Vilas Hall, but rather commonly on Langdon or State Street or in a co-ed's dorm at 4 a.m.; it's called life skills.

March 30, 2011

Thirty years ago, today, a five-year-old was bummed because *The Batman Movie* (1966) got preempted on Channel 11 WPIX. So glad that day didn't turn out like it could have.

"I hope all of you guys are Republicans. Honey, I forgot to duck." RIP Ronald Wilson Reagan.

April 5, 2011

I have been playing the drinking game where every time someone calls for Eric Holder's resignation, I do a shot. Today, I had a liver transplant.

April 12, 2011

In this time of devastating earthquakes and disasters, war in Libya, civil uprising and unrest in Syria, and the unending threat of government shutdown—please let us remember that there is nothing more important than William and Kate's wedding.

May 1, 2011

Welcome to hell, Bin Laden.

May 2, 2011

UBL dead. Chuck Schumer laments the expiration of the terrorist estate tax.

May 2, 2011

Bin Laden's death briefly interrupts omnipresent Facebook status of "cookies baked today."

May 2, 2011

UBL'S last tweet(s): "Chillin' at the mansion. Mad props to D-Wade and LBJ for taking care of the Celts. Allah is great. Hey, what was that noise?"

May 7, 2011(On Ex-Beatle's Wedding to Nancy Shevell)

Congrats, Paul McCartney. It's about time you got yourself a Conservative.

May 20, 2011

In preparation for tomorrow's Rapture, can everyone that owes me money pay me back ASAP?

July 9. 2011 (On Jeter's 3000th hit)

Second hit of the day at 2:00 p.m. for number two is his third homer for 3,000. Someone call Time Life Books.

July 21, 2011

This just in: A new Gallup poll shows that 89 percent of Americans think "cut, cap, and balance" is a new dance.

July 21, 2011

"The government that robs Peter to pay Paul can always count on Paul's support." —George Bernard Shaw

July 25, 2011 (On Obama's Speech)

Only a community agitator of the lowest common denominator goes on national television begging and pleading for people to clog up Congress's phone lines.

August 11, 2011

If you voted for Obama and now regret it, please paint a big red X on your front door so the revolution knows which homes to spare.

August 11, 2011

I can only assume that Ron Paul is the result of some Medicare Advantage anti-psychotic medication testing programs gone awry.

August 13, 2011

BO's cabinet members remind me of the bar scene in Star Wars.

August 14, 2011 (On Pawlenty Dropping Out of Presidential Race)

Don't let the door hit you in the ass, Pawlenty. You wanna get tough with girls, get a job at MSNBC.

August 26, 2011

Congrats to my Yanks for once again making history. Three Slams in One Game.

August 30, 2011 (On Darryl Hannah's Arrest)

Getting arrested to revive a sagging career? That's so Zsa Zsa circa 1989, Darryl Hannah.

August 31, 2011

BO ends vacation that started in January of 2009.

September 14, 2011 (On Yankee great, Mariano Rivera)

Congrats on save number 600, Mo.

September 18, 2011

Can the Emmy's suck any worse? Can't we just have a three-hour shot of Christina Hendricks?

October 10, 2011 (On Occupy Wall Street)

Fleabaggers infest Wall Street, thousands of parents' basements and community colleges empty. Film at 11 p.m.

October 28, 2011

Best World Series game in 23 years.

October 30, 2011 (On His World Series Failures)

Matt Holiday must pay for his championship ring.

November 1, 2011

Waiting for PETA to start protesting these "Messin' with Sasquatch" ads.

November 9, 2011 (On the Republican Debate)

Rick Perry, I'm guessing you didn't take a debate class in high school?

November 19, 2011 (On LAPD Reopening Investigation into Natalie Wood's Death)

The real reason 82 percent of Americans think America is on the wrong track is because the Natalie Wood case still triggers doubt and unrest. Thank you, LAPD, for trying to right this wrong and once again restore America's faith. While you're at it, could you please investigate the Fatty Arbuckle murder case from The Silent Era? America's sense of justice has no higher calling.

2012

January 15, 2012 (On NY Giants win in Playoffs during union strike)

Sayonara, progressive Packer fans. Get back to your bitching about collective bargaining agreements for illiterate union workers.

January 16, 2012

Breaking News: Huntsman to drop out of the race. Romney expected to pick up the all-important "I didn't vote" vote.

January 16, 2012

I just lost a $10,000 bet to Mitt Romney for 1993 wager that Dolly Parton and Queen Latifah would never team up for a big screen musical. Damn you, *Joyful Noise*, damn you to hell!

January 16, 2012 (On Packers Playoff Loss)

I'm Chris Hansen with Dateline, and if there's anything else you'd like to tell us, we're happy to hear it. If not, the Packers are free to leave the NFL.

January 16, 2012 (On Republican Primary Debate)

OK, Romney will release his tax returns when Ron Paul releases the list of anti-psychotic medications he's currently taking.

January 18, 2012 (On Italian Cruise Ship Disaster)

I am nominating that Italian ship captain for a cabinet post in BO's administration. He belongs with those criminals and creative tax cheats. "I didn't abandon ship. I slipped and fell into the lifeboat," he said. I love it.

January 20, 2012 (Republican Debate)

Here's to Newt for shredding King to pieces. Judgment for the mainstream media who protect and spread propaganda for our brainless dictator is coming soon.

January 22, 2012 (NFL Playoffs)

Attention, fans, please stay at Candlestick after the game, where you will be treated to a showing of *Moneyball* projected from Pam Oliver's forehead.

January 12, 2012

A Liberal Mugged

Last night, I broke into a Liberal's home. As I was rummaging through his wallet on his nightstand, he awoke, saw me confiscate his money, and exclaimed, "Hey, you are stealing from me!"

"No, I'm not," I replied, "I'm simply redistributing your wealth."

A few seconds later, the Liberal followed me as I entered his master bathroom. Once inside, I began pouring all his medications and pills into a sack I had brought with me.

"Hey pal, I paid for those pills. What the hell are you doing?" he said.

"No worries. I simply want to ensure that others can have equal access to healthcare." I stated.

Next, I found a cozy spot on the Liberal's large sofa in his living room. I promptly planted myself in the corner section.

"You need to leave now. You are trespassing," the Liberal shouted.

"I beg to differ, my friend. I am merely occupying your living room."

"I am calling the police." The now red-eared Liberal screamed.

"The pigs? Why?" I asked.

"Because you have seized what is not yours, completely indifferent to my private property rights and liberty. You seek to give others that which is not inherit but a privilege. You have annexed space that doesn't belong to you, and now you will face the due diligence of law enforcement for whom you seem to show no respect or deference!" Once he realized what he said, the Liberal crumbled slowly on the sofa. His eyes sparkled with an even marriage of amazement and chagrined understanding.

With a wry smile, I stood up, emptied the medicinal contents of the sack onto the living room table, returned the US currency to its rightful owner, and left the Liberal's home.

Once outside, I walked with haste to the next Liberal's home and thought, "There are many more people here in America that I need to teach; many more houses that I need to help. 2012 is going to be a busy year."

February 5, 2012 (On Super Bowl Halftime Performance by the Aging Madonna)

Wasn't that a great halftime show performance by Betty White?

February 5, 2012

BO just called the Giants and asked them to share the Lombardi trophy with the other 31 teams.

February 17, 2012

I noticed a rather cool anecdote was missing from all the Gary Carter coverage today. With two outs in the bottom of the ninth of Game Six and Gary Carter at-bat, the diamond vision at Shea Stadium briefly flashed the message, "Congratulations, Boston Red Sox —1986 World Champions."

March 3, 2012 (On New Orleans Saints Bounty Scandal)

I'm considering hiring the New Orleans Saints defense to take out Congress.

March 3, 2012 (On Sandra Fluke Controversy)

Nothing spells W-H-O-R-E more than testifying before Congress that you need $3,000 for birth control. This, combined with Taibbi's Rolling Stone blog on Breitbart's death and the corresponding comments thread, proves that Liberalism knows no bottom floor.

March 3, 2012

One bomb scare, and Limbaugh apologized to Sandra Floozie? Come on, you're better than that, Maha-Rushi.

March 5, 2012 (On the Portly Fox News Channel Political Analyst)

Karl Rove's image just floated out of my TV set and ate my entire dinner.

March 6, 2012

Hey, Karl Rove, put down the cheesesteak, wipe the grease off your chins and call Ohio for Santorum, you no good RINO you.

April 20, 2012

If anyone is interested in helping with the Annual Spring Pledge Drive for The New Black Panther Party, please message me.

May 4, 2012 (On Mariano Rivera's Injury)

Come on, Mo'. All of our prayers for a speedy recovery.

May 8, 2012

Attention all real estate agents. I realize many of you didn't even consider graduating from high school, so allow me to enlighten you. When showing a property, it might be a good idea to know little things like (1) property taxes, (2) HOA dues, (3) square footage, etc. I'm just sayin'

May 14, 2012

The FBI recently updated its' Top 10 Terrorists list. The number one spot? Yep, you guessed it, Morgan Fairchild.

June 7, 2012 (On a Visit to a Nearby Mall)

Food court time. Time to play, "Who's Closest to Giving Birth?"

"Oh, she looks like seven, maybe eight months." And her, "Wow, gotta be close to full term."

And "Oh, we have a winner. The chick in the Lynard Skynyrd tank top whose water just broke in front of the Orange Julius."

June 28, 2012 (On SCOTUS Obamacare Ruling)

For the past couple of years, the Dems have voiced their outrage for tax cuts for so-called millionaires and billionaires and decried increased tax burdens on middle-income earners. Today's ruling by SCOTUS clarifies Obamacare is the largest single tax increase on the middle class in history. Good luck running on this one for the next 100 years, Libs.

June 28, 2012 (ON SCOTUS' Unfortunate Obamacare Decision)

Apparently, Chief Justice Roberts hates going out in public.

June 28, 2012

I have a strong feeling that *The Pelican Brief* will be watched many times tonight.

August 16, 2012

"If you are not a Liberal at 20, you have no heart. If you are not a Conservative at 35, you have no brain." —Sir Winston Churchill

August 17, 2012

To all the intellectually dishonest, morally bereft buffoons who are viciously attacking Mitt Romney for his wealth, where were you in 2004 when John Kerry ran for president? Huh? Kerry's estimated fortune of $230.98 million dwarfs Romney's $150 million. True, Romney is not exactly out on the corner with a cup full of pencils, but at least he earned his money through hard work and not by gold-digging for wealthy widows. Yet not a peep from the Left about Kerry, Pelosi's wealth of $35 million, or Harry Reid's amassed fortune of over $10 million on an average annual salary of $170,000.

Reid has used his power and influence as Senate Majority Leader to fatten his wallet. He proposed building a bridge from Laughlin, Nevada, to Arizona because he owns 100 acres nearby. Furthermore, Reid sold his interest in stocks and funds comprised of energy and oil companies shortly before bringing to vote on the Senate floor a bill that heavily taxed energy-producing companies, thereby driving down their stock market value. Romney could have taken the easy way out and sat on his father's inheritance, but instead, he donated everything to charity. Charity. C-H-A-R-I-T-Y. Noun (a) organization which collects money to help the poor or support some cause (b) kindness (to the poor/the oppressed).

I supply Webster Dictionary's definition to educate Liberals, especially Joe "Gaffe Master" Biden himself. Crazy Joe spends so much time insulting African Americans that he doesn't have any left to be generous with his income. According to their 2011 tax returns, the Bidens earned $379,000 and gave a paltry $5,500 to charity. That's 1.46 percent. It turns out Crazy Joe is part of the 99 percent; it's just that he keeps 99 percent for himself and gives away the 1 percent.

Meanwhile, a 2006 study by Syracuse University found that Conservatives give about 30 percent more money per year to private charitable causes than Liberals despite being outearned by Liberals by about 6 percent. So much for the "evil, rich Conservative" mantra.

The same study showed that Conservatives donate more blood than Liberals every year. Although I think this speaks less to Conservatives' altruism and more to Liberals not being able to pass the pre-donation screening questions of "have you ever tried cocaine or heroin?" or "visited a brothel?"

August 17, 2012

OK, Mitt Romney will show his last five years' tax returns when Joe Biden shows his high school diploma. Deal?

August 17, 2012

After his hard-hitting interview with Entertainment Tonight, BO will appear with Michelle at the *Nickelodeon Kids Choice Awards*. Rumor has it they will be green slimed after answering, "I don't know," to Selena Gomez's questions about BO's comprehensive immigration reform policy.

August 21, 2012

When *Newsweek* does a story, telling BO it's time to go, you know he's in trouble. How much of a disaster does your presidency have to be for you to lose the support of the mindless minions in mainstream media?

With his friends deserting him one by one, BO did a radio interview with a New Mexico FM radio station where, I kid you not, he was asked the following questions:

"If you had a superpower, what would it be?

"What's your favorite New Mexican food?"

"What's your favorite song to work out to?"

While it's unclear how much time BO spent preparing his answers, word is he did not need a teleprompter. I'm guessing the interview came as a result of internal White House polling showing the Anointed One has lost ground among the all-important KOB-FM "*Morning Mayhem*" demographic.

I can just imagine the lead-in: "Welcome back to Albuquerque's hit station where caller number five will win Carly Rae Jepsen tickets, but first, the leader of the free world. Tell 'em how to do it, Barry."

"Ah, um. Call me. Maybe?"

August 21, 2012 (Reflection on BO's Roanoke Soliloquy)

"If you've got a business, you didn't build that. Somebody else made that happen." —Barack Hussein Obama, July 13, 2012, Roanoke, Virginia

Admittedly, I spent the first few weeks following BO's proclamation strongly perturbed at what he said, infuriated that the president of the United States could make such an incendiary, ridiculous, offensive comment aimed at the small business owners of our nation. How could the leader of the free world aim his always seemingly full vernacular revolver at those people who, through their sheer gumption, hard work, and dedication, have manufactured successful stories of capitalism which in turn have helped foster the backbone of our nation? But after some consideration, my attitude shifted from anger to sympathy. Yes, sympathy. For it was at this point that I realized that BO's attack was entirely out of jealousy. It's often said that when you criticize others, you're talking about yourself.

Case in point; BO.

I think the irony is that Obama's remarks are actually about himself. See, Obama's jabbing commentary about small business owners who have made it on their own came out of the realization that he's always needed the help of others. This epiphany has a man whose favorite color is red, turning green with envy.

Who but BO has achieved more undeserved success in life? Who has more than Barack Hussein Obama not gotten there "on their own?" Who but our current commander-in-grief has attained a greater level of success almost entirely owed to "somebody else?"

Here are just a few examples:

- Considering his lousy grades, Barack Obama did not get into Occidental College for undergrad on his own; Affirmative Action programs made that happen

- Barack Obama did not get accepted and transfer into Columbia University on his own; his dishonest and felonious status as a foreign exchange student made that happen

- Barack Obama did not become president of the United States on his own; the mainstream media made that happen

- Barack Obama did not kill Osama bin Laden on his own; the US Navy Seals made that happen. On a side note, according to a soon-to-be-released book, BO had thrice ruled against the Osama bin Laden kill raid before Secretary of State Hillary Clinton convinced him otherwise. I'm not sure Hillary knew who the intended target was, but rather, based on her life experiences, was just jumping at a chance to kill a man in bed with nine girls.

- Barack Obama did not exit the White House on January 29, 2013, on his own; the American voters made that happen

September 5, 2012

Tonight, I was an hour and a half into watching what I thought was Night of the Living Dead when I realized it was the DNC.

September 5, 2012

So, the DNC's keynote speaker is the mayor of a city that is trying to turn human waste into energy. Ironic since so many Democrats' ideas are a waste of human energy.

September 5, 2012

BO moved his DNC speech from Bank of America Stadium to a smaller venue due to so-called weather concerns. Yet another example of our commander-in-grief blaming others for his problems. The weather, he says. No BO, no one wants to hear your tired, ignorant, divisive rants on class-warfare, poverty-hustling, or Bush's so-called failures. There's only a 20 percent chance of inclement weather but a 100 percent chance of a mostly empty stadium. Much like an aging rocker whose time has also passed, BO is opting for a smaller, more intimate venue where his almost completely faded glory won't be as noticeable.

September 6, 2012

Breaking News: Former cop Drew Peterson found guilty of murdering his third wife. DNC has extended a speaking invitation to him for this evening.

September 7, 2012

So, to Michelle, her husband is still the guy that picked her up in a rusted-out car, wore shoes a half size too small, and whose favorite possession was a coffee table he found in the garbage. It looks like BO is a B-U-M.

September 12, 2012

Ambivalent about MLB's just-released 2013 schedule. Interleague play each day but some good ones like Dodgers at Yanks for the first time in the regular season since they left Brooklyn. Dodgers will also play host to Yanks. Astros in American League while Red Sox will move to International League.

September 12, 2012

Hard to believe it was Muslims responsible for yesterday's massacre in Libya. They have never before perpetrated an act of violence unless you count 9/11, the simultaneous bombings of the US embassies in Kenya and Tanzania, the attack on the U.S.S. Cole, the hijacking of the Achille Lauro, the US Marines truck bombing in Beirut, the Rome and Vienna airport attacks, the Bali bombing, the Berlin discotheque bombing, the 72 Munich games, Pan Am Flight 103, The Ft. Hood massacre, the first World Trade Center bombing, the US Embassy in Tehran, the murder of Daniel Pearl, Black Hawk Down, the Tel Aviv Bus suicide attack, the London train bombings, the Mumbai bombings of 2006, etc., etc., etc. But apart from that, not much, just 18,000 separate attacks since 2001 alone. Remember, kids, Islam is a religion of peace.

September 14, 2012

I love how there is a Middle Eastern dating connection commercial here in Atlanta. "Hey, are you single and have thought of bombing Buckhead?"

September 18, 2012

These are just a couple of excerpts from the recent Joe Biden Twitter (@ loopyvp) Q&A chat.

"Twitter? Twitter, huh? Sounds like something a clean, articulate, Black man would say at a Dunkin Donuts in Delaware."

Is it just me, or is Richard Gere still totally fuckable? There, I said it. So, sue me, Holder. (Even odder since this was in response to a question about China manipulating their currency)

September 25, 2012

Obama, NFL replacement referees, Facebook IPO, and Joy Behar is still alive. I hope that Mayan Calendar thingy pans out after all.

October 1, 2012 (On "Fast and Furious")

Obama/Biden 2012 Slaughtering innocent Mexican civilians since 2009.

October 3, 2012 (On Upcoming Presidential Debate)

Promoters are billing tonight's debate as:

"The Man from Bain against the Man with No Brain."

"The Fracas over Higher Taxes."

"The Stormin' Mormon vs. Body Blow BO"

At the weigh-in, Obama vowed to re-distribute Romney's face all over Colorado while Romney guaranteed he would kick 99 percent of Obama's ass. Will the notorious glass-jawed Obama withstand the Romney right hook that KO'ed Perry, Gingrich, and Santorum? Or will Romney show all the defense of an American consulate in Libya on the anniversary of 9/11, hence being susceptible to Obama's Far-left jabs, which he always seems to teleprompt, I mean telegraph? One thing is for sure; Joe Biden is insane.

Tune in tonight at 9 p.m. for this epic battle. SAP everywhere. Closed Captioning available. Or tune into MSNBC, where they will dub Obama's remarks into Arabic.

October 3, 2012 (Presidential Debate)

BO is getting wiped on the floor by Romney. Meanwhile, Lehrer looks like an old principal trying to stop a butt whooping in the lunchroom unsuccessfully.

October 3, 2012 (Presidential Debate)

Game over. BO just admitted that healthcare costs have gone up with Obamacare.

October 3, 2012

In the mid-1970s, Tina Turner had more control over Ike Turner than Jim Lehrer had over this bloodbath tonight.

October 3, 2012

Obama would like to thank his debate coach, Rick Perry.

October 3, 2012

What kind of a wuss begs the moderator to move on to a different topic when he's getting his butt kicked? "Teacher, the smart boy is picking on me again."

October 3, 2012

To compensate for tonight's "Massacre in the Mountains," all the pollsters will have to up their over-sampling of Democrats from +13 to +40 to make polls look good.

October 3, 2012

With all that's happened tonight following the monumental debate, let us not forget to congratulate my Yanks on yet another American League East Title.

October 3, 2012

Congrats also to Miguel Cabrera, baseball's first triple crown winner in 45 years!

October 4, 2012 (On Miggy, Triple Crown married with Fast N' Furious)

When asked about Miguel Cabrera tonight, BO responded, "You mean one of the guys Holder killed with our guns?"

October 4, 2012 (On Facebook IPO)

I'm so effin' pumped. Reverend Jeremiah Wright just accepted my friend request. Here's what he just posted on my page: "Not God Bless Marc Zuckerberg, God Da*n Marc Zuckerberg! My IPOs in the toilet. It's in the Bible! He was ridin' dirty with those two twins at Harvard. Myspace's Chickens comin' home to roost."

October 5, 2012 (On Phony Jobs Report)

This morning's jobs report will undoubtedly fool Obama's uneducated, unsuspecting base. But what else do you expect from the great unwashed masses who want their "Obama phone" and "don't gotta worry about payin' for gas or my mortgage anymore?" To understand that for not one day in Obama's presidency were there as many Americans working as under Bush? That the jobs number does not account for the number of Americans who work part-time or are no longer looking for work? That it gets revised downward every month? I'm sure the details of U-6 job numbers are too mentally cumbersome for the intellectually bereft buffoons. They wouldn't know an alarm clock from a non-government-provided contraceptive because they haven't touched either.

October 5, 2012 (On Phony Jobs Report)

Today's government-tinkered, synthetically manufactured jobs report reminded me of something else; Saddam Hussein's last "electoral" victory, where he won 99.9 percent of the vote.

October 5, 2012 (On Phony Jobs Report)

No, no, no, Mr. Obama, please allow me to guess what your doctored October jobs report will be, henceforth known as "Doctober," due for release just four days before the election. "The nation's unemployment rate dropped from 7.8 percent to 0.0 percent. Employers added 24 million jobs in October. All comrades are employed."

October 16, 2012 (On Facebook's New Policy to Make a Buck)

You can now promote an "important post" for seven dollars. No thanks.

October 16, 2012 (On the Presidential Debate)

BO could show up tonight with a swastika tattooed on his forehead and pass out on top of Candy Crowley before uttering a single word, and the mainstream media would still hail him as the victor. Mark my words, folks, the "Comeback Kid" story has already been written in the minds, if not the PCs of the Liberal elites.

October 16, 2012 (On Presidential Debate – BO's Take on College-Educated Kids Getting Manufacturing Jobs)

So, you see, Jeremy, when you graduate from college, a manufacturing job will be waiting for you.

October 16, 2012

I like that Mitt stood when they arrived while BO chose to remain seated on a stool. It made him look small and weak.

October 16, 2012

Amazingly, they allowed Candy Crowley to slow-roast a rack of lamb while moderating tonight.

October 16, 2012 (On Questions from the Audience Full of New Yorkers)

Could the accents be any worse? I mean, come on. This is like half-price Gefiltefish Day at Liebman's.

October 16, 2012

Good for you, Mitt. Stay tough in this two-to-one battle. Though with Candy, it's more like three-to-one.

October 16, 2012

So let me get this straight, low gas prices are bad because they mean the economy is in the gutter. BO really knows how to connect with the middle class struggling to fill their tanks.

October 16, 2012

Earth to BO, capital gains taxes are low to encourage investments, dummy.

October 16, 2012

A tax cut does not "cost" anything. It's not the government's money; it's the people's money. How about you stop spending like Lindsey Lohan's father during a full moon?

October 16, 2012

Candy would sooner leave an Olive Garden breadstick on the table before she would dare interrupt BO.

October 16, 2012

After all these audience plants, the next question will likely be from Jay Carney.

October 16, 2012

The flow of illegals is lower because there are no jobs here in the US, not because of your imaginary strict border policy, BO. The only thing you know about the border is the number of guns you send across it into Mexico.

October 16, 2012

BO believes in the free enterprise system the way Candy believes in the Atkins diet.

October 16, 2012

Candy calls the Libya Rose Garden question in BO's favor. Can we all now see Erick Erickson as the RINO that he is? Just days ago, he was praising Candy and thought she would be a fair moderator.

October 16, 2012

Mitt Romney was tough and factual. He didn't let BO filibuster with his incessant falsehoods. The second debate goes to Mitt but not by as wide a margin as the first.

October 16, 2012

Oh, AOL is going to fact check tonight's debate. Wonderful. I hope this mental exercise won't take away too much time from their crack staff editors' duties of arranging slide shows of Lindsey Lohan's mug shots or links to Michelle Obama's garden photos.

October 17, 2012

Candy "Bar" Crowley needs to walk back her comment about Libya. Wrong. Wrong. Wrong.

October 17, 2012

Romney is up by six points in the latest Gallup poll. This means the Chicago thugs will have to work extra hard to steal the election.

October 17, 2012

So, the would-be Federal Reserve bomber sought to destroy the US economy. I guess he didn't realize BO already beat him to it.

October 19, 2012 (On Traditional Alfred Smith Dinner)

Consider, if you will, last night's Alfred Smith dinner in NYC as Romney-Obama appearance 2-A. Romney appeared presidential, stately, and well-coiffed. He was as comfortable in his ability to poke fun at himself as he was in his zingers toward the president. He exuded an aura of confidence in his demeanor, befitting the leader of the free world. Add to this his impeccable comedic timing married with his now famous ability to deadpan during a punchline, and he had America thinking, "Wow. Romney is nothing like the portrait painted of him in those attack ads."

In contrast, BO appeared uneasy, stiff, and awkward. He fumbled the setup lines to self-deprecating jokes that were written for him and looked very much as he did in the first debate, like he didn't want to be there. Despite being afforded the plum positioning of speaking after Romney, BO appeared every bit the opening act instead of the headliner. Could it be that he now realized, as America is starting to, that he has no business being on the same stage as Romney? That he looks small in comparison? Weak? I think so.

A piece of advice to the Romney campaign: challenge BO to a fourth debate. Call it a debate, a discussion, a non-alcoholic beer summit, whatever. Just make sure that both Romney and Obama appear someplace together engaged in a discussion of ideas. It's a win-win for Romney. If B.O. and his Chicago thug cronies refuse, America will interpret it as fear. If they agree, Romney has another chance to destroy the faux leader of "Hope and Change."

October 22, 2012 (On Third and Last Presidential debate)

The only thing Mitt needs to say in tonight's foreign policy debate is, "Libya."

October 22, 2012

A sitting president always has the edge in a debate on foreign policy because he has all the "intelligence" (even if he skipped the meetings like BO). Let's remember, four years ago, Obama's only foreign policy experience was being born in Kenya.

October 22, 2012

Let's face it, America, even Dr. Brown and Marty McFly handled the Libyans better than BO.

October 22, 2012

Hats off to Bob Schieffer for taking time off from his "Metamucil and *Murder, She Wrote* hour" to be tonight's token Liberal moderator. Don't you go dyin' on me now.

October 22, 2012

Schiefer has moderated two other presidential debates: Lincoln/Douglas and then, years later on his 105th birthday, Dewey/Truman.

October 22, 2012

When BO talks about Israel being an ally, his body language displays several signs of deception.

October 22, 2012

BO just called for "nation building" back home. For once, I concur entirely with him.

October 27, 2012

I just voted early in Atlanta, much to the local Liberal base's chagrin, who are unaccustomed to living balloters not named "Mickey Mouse."

October 29, 2012 (On Superstorm Sandy)

Hearts and prayers to all my family and friends in the Northeast.

October 31, 2012

So, several months from now, will ex-president BO be telling New Jerseyans, "Hey, you didn't rebuild that?"

November 2, 2012 (On Superstorm Sandy Benefit Concert)

Bon Jovi is performing at the benefit? Haven't those poor Sandy victims suffered enough?

November 2, 2012

Estimates to repair Sandy damages run as high as $50 billion do. How can China afford this?

November 2, 2012

Six-trillion-dollars in new debt, one out of every seven Americans on food stamps, 23 million Americans can't find jobs, the seventh-largest tax hike on middle class Americans in history (Obamacare), the first downgrade of our nation's credit rating, cries from our consulate in Libya ignored and four Americans killed including our ambassador, average family household income down over $4,400, gas prices doubling the last four years, Israel ignored, Iran continues unfettered on the path to nuclear weapons, chaos in Syria and Egypt, bowing to despots, apologizing on behalf of America's history. Yeah, I want four more years of this.

November 3, 2012

On November 4, 2008, the Real Clear Politics (RCP) seven-day poll average had Obama at 52.1 percent and McCain at 44.5 percent. The final results of that election showed Obama at 51.38 percent and McCain at 46.80 percent. Much closer for McCain than the RCP seven-day poll averages showed.

On November 3, 2012, the RCP seven-day average had Obama at 47.4 percent and Romney at 47.3 percent. Given the fact that most 2012 polls are using 2008 voter turnout models, these numbers are heavily skewed toward Democrats. No one in their right mind thinks that Democrat turnout will mirror 2008; even actual early voting turnout is showing that.

All of this bodes well for Governor Romney on Election Day, especially when you consider the fact that McCain won the same day as election voting. It all comes down to Ohio and their much-coveted 18 electoral votes, you say? Perhaps.

November 3, 2012

The one silver lining in this tough week, Mo's back!

November 3, 2012

How come it always looks like the sign language interpreter next to Bloomberg communicates a different message than what he's saying? How do we know she's not signing statements like, "I can't believe how short this guy is." or "Really? Thank you, Mayor Munchkin, for outlawing salty food, oversized Big Gulps and anything taller than you."

November 5, 2012

A CNN poll has Romney and Obama tied at 49 percent, but they had to over-sample Democrats by 11 points to make it look good. Most of these Liberal polls are laughable. Will everyone who hasn't yet please vote tomorrow?

November 5, 2012

BO says if he loses tomorrow (more like when he loses tomorrow), he will not run for the White House in 2016. Quiz: Who is the only president in US history to serve two non-consecutive terms?

November 5, 2012

New Hampshire's Motto: Live Free or Die. Apparently, the state is evenly divided on this.

November 6, 2012 (On CT Senate Race)

Linda McMahon loses Senate bid in CT. Chris Murphy takes folding chair to the back of the head.

November 15, 2012

I'm tired of all these pundits saying that we can expect Petraeus to testify truthfully tomorrow because he is a "very honest man." Hello? He had to resign because he was caught cheating on his wife.

November 17, 2012

Since the election, there have been massive lay-offs due to Obamacare; Israel is at war, no more Twinkies, The Benghazi Mess, Unemployment Claims up, Dow is down big. And just think, his second term hasn't even started yet.

December 1, 2012

Here's my proposal to keep everyone happy: Since BO and the Libs are hell-bent on letting the Bush-Era tax cuts expire for the top 2 percent of earners so they can collect an extra 80 billion in taxes (heavy on the sarcasm here) to help run our government for only eight and a half days, let's have the House majority Republican leadership (and I use the word "leadership" loosely here) agree to that "revenue" by confiscating the entire net worth of one Bill Gates. Gates is the richest man in the world, and his net worth is approaching $80 billion.

Both sides can agree to extend tax cuts for all income brackets because they found a way to collect BO's much sought-after revenue through one very wealthy, Liberal man. The 100 percent confiscation of Mr. Gates' wealth would satisfy BO's ironic hatred of big business, many of which are his biggest donors. It would also validate his now famous (or infamous) "You Didn't Build That" speech in Roanoke, Virginia.

Is there a better example of someone who owes their success to another person than Bill Gates? If it weren't for his habitual theft of Steve Jobs's ideas, Gates would have been just another Seattle-area college dropout working as a Starbucks barista and living in his parents' basement. Ironically, I am currently typing this on Android —I am so sorry, Stevie!

"But, Mr. Hilway," you say, "that only covers one year."

True. That's why I would like to submit more Liberal names for future consideration in the "100 percent wealth confiscation lottery." Warren Buffett, Oprah, every Hollywood star, Nancy Pelosi, John Kerry, most of the NBA, and the list goes on and on. Of course, many of these people would have to be combined in given years to reach the much-coveted revenue for eight-and-a-half days of government. The Libs always say the rich should pay their fair share and be patriotic; here is their chance to prove it.

December 4, 2012 (On Bob Costas Getting Political During Broadcasts)

Be sure to tune into this week's NBC *Sunday Night Football* game, Detroit vs. Green Bay, where Bob Costas will discuss Aaron Rodgers, Coach Jim Schwartz's job security, and Roe Vs. Wade at halftime.

December 5, 2012

The New Orleans Pelicans? Really? Just because this is the age of Obama, does everything need to be sissified?

December 7, 2012 (On Another Phony Jobs report)

Today, I am calling for the swift, public execution of all those who believe the job numbers.

December 7, 2012

BO's speech today on the anniversary of Pearl Harbor:

"My fellow Americans, 71 years ago today, we witnessed the second-worst case of 'workplace violence' in our history. As tragic as the attack on Pearl Harbor by a small minority of misunderstood Asians was, I agree with my good friend, Bob Costas. Those 2,402 Americans would have been alive on December 8, 1941, had it not been for the Imperial Japanese Navy's invention of the Mitsubishi A6M2 Zero carrier fighter. Today, I would like to apologize for the past internment of our Japanese citizens in several camps on the West Coast. This gross act not only robbed them of their constitutional rights but, more importantly, led to the loss of government revenues these "one-per-centers" could have supplied, thereby fulfilling their patriotic duties. I would like to close on a personal note. The state of Hawaii is a place near and dear to my heart. It's where I pretend I was born and where to this day, many forged documents of my birth still reside. Thank you all, and God Bless the Land of The Rising Sun, second only to the People's Republic of China in the amount of debt the US owes."

2013

January 3, 2013

A very happy, belated 50th birthday to one of my favorite Yanks ever, David Cone.

Now here's something weird, wild, wacky, and very spooky. Coney is one of just three players to pitch a perfect game in Yankees history. He accomplished the feat on July 18, 1999, at the old Yankee Stadium. Don Larsen threw out the ceremonial first pitch that day. Larsen threw a perfect-o for the Yanks in the 1956 World Series; the only perfect game in MLB post-season history. Larsen attended Point Loma High School in San Diego. Guess who else went there? That's right, David Wells, who rounds out the list of Yankees to pitch perfect games.

The next time the Yanks had a nearly perfect game was September 2, 2001. Mike Mussina was one strike away from making history at Fenway Park against the Boston Red Sox when notorious sociopath Carl Everett hit an opposite-field single. The Sox starting pitcher that night was David Cone. Weird, I know.

January 4, 2013

If anyone wants to see a microcosm of the result of 100 years of "progressive" policies by the Libs, all they have to do is visit the food court at the Willowbrook Mall in Wayne, NJ.

January 5, 2013

So, Al Gore wanted to sell his TV network before December 31 to avoid paying higher taxes? Please welcome the latest Lib hypocrite to join the "Closet Supply-Side Economics" club. While we're at it, let's remind the brain-dead Lefties that Al-Jazeera is a network that makes their money from oil profits. Gore has made more money from oil than Bush or Cheney ever did. Where are the Lefties on this one? So much for Mr. Global Warming. Not only does he fly in G-6 planes and ride around in gas-guzzling SUVs, but he also doesn't see a problem from "profiteering" (yes, I am hijacking a term from the Far-left loon dictionary) of the oil trade. Gotta love the Left's integrity.

January 9, 2013 (On Brent Musburger QB GF drama)

Being referred to as a "beautiful woman" on national television is not an "ordeal."

January 13, 2013 (On Pete Carroll's Coaching Debacle)

Seriously, how drunk was Pete Carroll today? In the state of Georgia, is it legal to forcibly withdraw blood from someone if they refuse a breathalyzer? I guess every day is St. Patrick's Day for ol' Pete. The lowlight of the day for

"Four-Pint" Pete was when he projectile vomited all over sideline reporter Laura Okmin after she asked him, "Do you know where you are?" and "How many fingers am I holding up?"

Are you kidding me? Thanks for ruining my man Russell's rookie season. No worries, Russell will be back; Pete won't.

January 18, 2013 (On Manti Te'o Debacle)

Look, there is nothing more important in the world at all right now than the Manti Teo story. I want all news and mention of gun control, taxation, our national debt, and Middle East conflicts put aside until we get to the bottom of "Mantigate." Priorities, people. The fact that this was the lead news story tonight is proof that (fill in the blank).

January 30, 2013 (On the Return of Ray Lewis to the Super Bowl)

Ray Lewis set to commemorate Super Bowl by stabbing to death an innocent bystander at a local sports bar.

February 1, 2013

RIP, Mayor Koch. One of the few Dems I had the utmost respect for.

February 2, 2013

New Secretary of Mistake, John "Theresa Heinz Ketchup" Kerry said, "I'm very anxious to get to work. I'll be reporting Monday morning at 9 o'clock to do my part."

Geez, John, don't let those brutal start hours get to you. Nice to know most Americans have a longer workday than our foremost ambassador. Also, John F. Kerry might want to avoid military-style phrases like "reporting" since he was swift boated so badly during the 2004 election for "reporting" on his fellow soldiers on Capitol Hill in 1971.

February 2, 2013

A Day in The Life of Chuck Hagel

7:00 a.m. - Hagel awakens to his alarm clock book on tape audio of "Mein Kampf."

7:14 a.m. - Within 15 seconds, he breaks his record for the quickest Anti-Semitic slur of the day, trashing his personal best, which he set back in 1953 when Julius and Ethel Rosenberg were executed for espionage.

8:00 a.m. - While muttering over breakfast porridge, he listens to his staff try to explain last night's episode of "Buckwild."

8:30 a.m. - He tells the chief of staff he is reporting back for "nappy time."

10 a.m. - During the Secretary of Defense confirmation hearings, he bungles the opening remarks by "wishing to thank that nice colored boy who nominated me."

Noon - During his lunch break, while intending to ask for the salt-shaker, he shouts, "Will somebody please pass the damn Jewish lobby?"

4 p.m. - Concludes hearing by asking if there is anyone he has yet to defend.

4:05 p.m. - Before the final gavel of day, he ends the hearing, grabs the microphone, and breaks into a bizarre rant about Pete Carrol's coaching deficiencies during the NFC Divisional playoff game before chagrined staffers drag him away.

6 p.m. - Over dinner, his staff tries once again to explain last night's episode of "Buckwild."

7 p.m. - Calls a Domino's Pizza in Jerusalem and has 750 pies sent to the home of Israeli Prime Minister Benjamin Netanyahu.

7:30 p.m. - Bedtime.

February 3, 2013 (On Super Bowl Blackout)

What the hell just happened? Katrina issues still? You're doing a heck of a job, Brownie. This is obviously Bush's fault. He has only done a fly-over here in New Orleans so far. Where is BO? How about FEMA? There are football fans without electricity to melt cheese on their nachos!

Don't worry, Steve Tasker to the rescue, everybody. Great, a power outage during the Super Bowl. What's next, a perpetually democratically controlled political class that decides to build a major US city one mile below sea level? They can get power back in 15 minutes in New Orleans, but people are still waiting for it in parts of the East Coast post-Sandy.

The lights go off, two people scream, and the lights then come back on with Ray Lewis holding a bloody knife. The butler did it at the Super Bowl with a pipe.

NFL Champion Baltimore Ravens to visit the White House.
Obama to Ray Lewis: "How did you get in here? Get past security clearance?"
Ray Lewis: "I was going to ask you the same question."

February 4, 2013 (On Super Bowl Aftermath)

Shannon Sharpe asked Ray Lewis whether this was truly his final game or not.

"I might come back for one more stabbing. I mean season. Season, that's what I meant to say."

February 4, 2013

"No wun needs 10 buhl-lets to kill ah deer!"

I'm not posting this to voice my position on this hotly debated topic. Both sides make great points, and this is one issue I am rather ambivalent on, but rather to make fun of Cuomo's ridiculously hilarious accent. His ambition to occupy 1600 Pennsylvania Avenue came crashing down in one fell swoop. Someone who sounds like this should be making bagel deliveries out of a cube truck at 5 a.m. in Staten Island, not running a state.

February 6, 2013

If Fox News takes yet another recent hard turn to the Left and hires Scott Brown, Murdoch and Ailes can kiss my ass goodbye.

February 12, 2013 (Eagerly awaited BO SOTU)

Pelosi's stitches just popped during an attempted smile.

Is there any truth in the rumor that Chris Dorner wrote parts of BO's speech tonight?

BO telling me about deficit reduction is like Peter O'Toole telling me about the virtues of a clean liver.

Really? Actually, healthcare premiums have gone up, BO.

How drunk is Boehner? Every time he mouth-vomits tonight, we all take a shot.

OK, I will start doing something about climate change when the University of East Anglia stops falsifying its research about it. Deal, BO?

China is "all in" on cleaner energy? I don't even think he believes the bullshit on his prompter.

I pray to God that Dr. Ben Carson approaches the stage, grabs the microphone, and intercedes.

Everyone is nervously waiting for the gun control part of the speech when cameras find Ted Nugent.

When you raise the minimum wage, you cost low-income workers jobs. Don't you get that?

Boehner is non-stop comedy tonight.

I think Boehner just yelled out, "God created Adam and Eve, not Adam and Steve," before quietly passing out into Plugs Biden's arms.

Supreme Court Justices Kagan and Sotomayor are excitedly looking at their watches, hoping he wraps this up before the *Cagney & Lacey* marathon begins.

It is a shame that some people had to wait six hours to have their vote changed to Obama/Biden.

Now's the part when US congressmen rush to the front row of the chamber for the chance to get an autograph from the president. Is this the end of the SOTO in the greatest country in the world or spring training?

February 12, 2013 (On State of the Union Focus Group Polling)

Tonight's Frank Lutz focus group identifies the problem with America and its voters. Nearly all had a favorable impression of BO's miserable "let's grow the deficit" State of the Union, but only half had a good impression of Rubio's heartfelt and brilliant response. Since we live in a society where drinking water in the middle of a speech usurps the negativity of the generational theft of your children and grandchildren, the American people will deservedly get their comeuppance and that right soon.

February 17, 2013

The NBA All-Star game is on? There used to be a day and time when I would know when this event occurred, and I cared about it. How times change.

So, the NFL champion Baltimore Ravens play-by-play guy is named Gerry Sandusky. Why didn't I know this until today?

February 18, 2013

According to KTLA, Mindy McCreedy will be charged posthumously for shooting and killing Christopher Dorner.

February 20, 2013 (On Jesse Jackson Jr.'s Legal Issues)

Now, this is comedy! Get to the part about him not wanting a trial because he doesn't want to waste the taxpayer's money. LMAO! I do admire Jackson Jr.'s passion for Rolex watches, but a mink cashmere cape and some Bruce

Lee memorabilia have me thinking "Pimp Walk" not "Perp Walk" I guess now we know how he built his wealth and don't need to read his 1999 book on the subject.

March 7, 2013

Tonight, an Oval Office-ordered predator drone attack killed my next-door neighbor in Atlanta, GA. According to AG Eric Holder, his crime was claiming too many Class-C itemized deductions on his tax return and illegally hook-up free Cinemax. If it can happen to him, it can happen to anyone. Wake up, America.

I was 20 minutes into what I thought was an episode of *The Golden Girls* when I realized it was a San Antonio Spurs game. Damn, Parker, Ginobili, and Duncan have aged.

March 7, 2013 (On Rand Paul's All Night Speech)

It's a PaulNighter, baby!

Rand Paul, there has not been a person gain this much late-night respect since Johnny Carson.

From now on, I will only answer to Rand Hilway.

March 7, 2013 (On Yankees injuries)

This spring training, the Yankees team photo will be an x-ray.

March 9, 2013

Did you ever notice that Boehner always speaks like he is stifling a Miller Lite belch?

March 13, 2013

A Pope forced to abdicate. We will see who the Bilderbergs choose.

April 5, 2013 (On Rutgers Homophobic Scandal)

In an effort to change its image, Rutgers University has hired Barney Frank as the new men's basketball head coach.

April 13, 2013

I might have had the stupidest waitress of all time.
Me: "I'll have one for the road."
Her: "We can't do that. You have to drink it here."
And she wasn't kidding.

April 15, 2013 (On Boston Marathon Bombing)

Hearts and prayers to those in Boston!

April 17, 2013

Listening to John King and Wild Blitzer on CNN fret over the fact that the suspect is a "dark-skinned individual." SMH

April 19, 2013

If CCN's John King had reported in Dallas on 11/22/63, he would have had it from two credible sources that Jackie Kennedy was in police custody and had been charged with the death of her husband, JFK.

Hats off to the Boston PD, the FBI, and other law enforcement officials involved in the apprehension of this animal.

April 24, 2013

George remembers a simpler time in American life when welfare recipients spent their Obama checks carelessly on tattoos, gambling, alcohol, and weed. Now, these crazy kids are using their government largesse to buy pressure cookers and nails to kill those that work for a living. How I long for the old days of the financially unmotivated blue-staters as opposed to the terrorist-minded blue-staters. MEM-OR-IES, of the way we were!

April 25, 2013

Mayor "Doomsberg" is a riot. It's unclear whether he's more enraged that the Boston Marathon bombers' next intended attack was Times Square or that they consumed Big Gulps at a 7-Eleven in Cambridge. "As bad as the death toll could have been in Times Square, let's not forget the damage 64 ounces of high fructose corn syrup, white processed sugar, and phosphoric acid is doing to young Dzhokhar Tsarnaev," he said to Reuters.

April 29, 2013 (On Jason Collins Coming Out as Gay)

I'm sure I won't be the only NBA fan going on YouTube tonight and looking for old footage of Jason Collins posting up against John Amaechi to see if the refs missed some "hanky-panky," if you know what I'm talking about.

June 19, 2013

I just heard the news. I'm devastated. *The Sopranos* was my favorite show of all time. RIP James Gandolfini

Much like the assassination of John Lennon in 1980 ended endless speculation of a Beatles reunion, so too will James Gandolfini's passing bring rest to the many calls for a *Sopranos* return.

Gandolfini's death comes nearly five years to the day that Tim Russert suffered a fatal heart attack after recently returning from Italy. Doctors caution that long flights can be dangerous to those with cardiovascular ailments.

June 22, 2013 (On Gandolfini Coincidence)

I just sat down at my favorite Italian restaurant in Atlanta, and "Don't Stop Believing" started to play. I swear to God.

June 28, 2013 (On Aaron Hernandez Arrest)

Aaron Hernandez was questioned by homicide detectives in connection to 36 unsolved murders in Boston dating back to the 1950s.

San Francisco and Vallejo PD's want extradition for Aaron Hernandez to California as new evidence shows he may be the elusive Zodiac Killer.

Aaron Hernandez, responsible for one-half of all Confederacy deaths during the US Civil War, says Defense Secretary Chuck Hagel.

In his poem entry into this year's Walt Whitman Poetry Contest, former Patriots player Aaron Hernandez wrote, "Every morning I see the sun, the flowers, and the birds and I know God must exist. But then at 5 p.m. clock after a couple of 40s, I wanna fuckin' kill all that shit!"

July 3, 2013

Obama wants to wait until after the midterms to implement the employer coverage part of his huge healthcare overhaul. I thought this was an integral part of his plan and would be a giant benefit to employees? Ah, the stupid American Democratic voter, always banana-slipping face-first into the ignorance cake at the Layman's Ball.

July 13, 2013

George Zimmerman not guilty: I believe the jury reached the only logical verdict they could.

July 19, 2013

What's up with people who don't wish you a "Happy Birthday" on here, but then "Like" your comment where you thank everyone for their birthday wishes? That's akin to Costanza's girlfriend taking credit for the "Big Salad."

July 20, 2013

Breaking News: Taylor Swift is now dating Trayvon Martin's hoodie. "Traylor," as low- information voter outpost, *Entertainment Tonight*, dubbed them, was spotted at a convenience store. The songstress was playfully wrapping the young dead man's hoodie around her waist and singing a song that was probably mocking John Mayer. Page Six sources overheard the obnoxious clerk ask if she wanted any skittles or tea, to which the pop-star reportedly replied, "Why you gotta be so mean?"

July 21, 2013

The best and most succinct way I can transcribe all of BO's speeches to the American public on the "benefits" of Obamacare is, "Who are you going to believe, me or your lying eyes?"

July 23, 2013 (On the Brewers Slugger PED story)

Ryan Braun reminds me so much of Jay Carney.

July 23, 2013

FYI from now on, I will only respond to "Carlos Danger."

August 14, 2013

In times of trouble and doubt, I'm always soothed by the words of ex-Yankee closer Rich "Goose" Gossage. While recalling his thoughts before facing Carl Yastrzemski in the ninth inning of New York's one game playoff victory over the Red Sox in 1978, he said, "the worst thing that can happen is that we lose the game and tomorrow I'm back in Colorado hunting and fishing."

August 16, 2013 (On the Coldest Atlanta Summer Day)

So, did all of my fellow Atlantans enjoy the first day of winter?

August 17, 2013

"The coldest winter I ever spent was the summer I spent in San Francisco."
—American humorist and author Mark Twain

"The Coldest winter I ever spent was the day I spent in Atlanta, August 16, 2013." —George Hilway

"It's cold in Atlanta!"

"How cold is it?"

"It's so cold in Atlanta that all of Obama's supporters are begging for spare change indoors."

September 2, 2013

Will someone please explain what Labor Day is to all the Obama voters?

September 26, 2013

Breaking News: MLB Commissioner Bud Selig to retire.

"Our long, national nightmare is over," said George Hilway.

September 30, 2013

New law: if your city receives a federal bailout, your pro sports team is automatically ineligible for the post-season. Sorry, Detroit Tigers.

(On Obama's Coziness with the Terrorist Nation)

If the House GOP wants BO to consider their proposals, they will have to give them to Iran to pass on.

October 11, 2013

Kris "Ex-Kardashian" Humphries responded to Adrian Peterson's two-year-old son's aggravated assault by his mother's boyfriend by tweeting, "Violence is never the answer."

Stupidest tweet ever. I guess in case there are still some people out there who are undecided about whether putting a two-year-old in the hospital in critical condition with head injuries might be considered an "answer."

October 29, 2013

Here's to Jay Carney-the stupidest member of the Obama administration-which is akin to being the craziest Jackson or the sleaziest Kardashian.

November 2, 2013

So, BO just proclaimed to the NRA that if "they like their gun, they can keep their gun." Should they be worried?

November 23, 2013 (On Yankees' Jacoby Ellsbury Signing)

Yankees and Cashman, are you friggin' kidding me? That money would have better been spent on signing me.

I just got done TP'ing Cashman's house. Man, that felt good.

December 4, 2013

Breaking News. Yankees and Grady Sizemore agree to a 15-year, $300 million deal with vesting option for a 16th season at $25 million.

Yankee GM Brian Cashman said, "It's been a busy off-season for us, and we can't wait for Grady to take his rightful place on the Disabled List next to Brian McCann and Jacoby Ellsbury as soon as possible."

Sizemore, who hasn't played in the Majors since 2011 with the Cleveland Indians, has missed 438 games since the 2009 season.

"It's those kinds of constant injuries that got our attention," stated Yankee principal owner and managing general partner Hal Steinbrenner. "With this addition, we have a lineup that has the potential to miss 1000 games."

At press time, the Yankees have released their 2014 home schedule. "X-Ray Night," where the first 5000 fans who bring in a recent x-ray of a broken bone will receive actual bone chip fragments of players from the 2013 injury-riddled season, will take place on April 20 in the Yankee game against their hated rivals, the Boston Red Sox.

December 6, 2013

Breaking News: Yankees to sign Nelson Mandela's corpse.

AP-NY-- In an unexpected move, the New York Yankees are set to sign the corpse of the late, former South African president and civil rights warrior, Nelson Mandela, sources close to the team say. Mandela, who passed away yesterday at the age of 95, is expected to be moved to Major League Baseball's Bereavement List. The terms of the deal are not known and calls to Mandela's agent, Jay-Z, were not immediately returned. The agreement is contingent upon Mandela passing an autopsy.

The move is the latest in what has been a very busy off-season for the "Bronx Bombers," in which they are aggressively attempting to mitigate the number of games their free agent signings will play in. Apparently not entirely happy with the recent acquisitions of Brian McCann and Jacoby Ellsbury's, the Yankees began to pursue Mandela as soon as news of the longtime imprisoned apartheid combatant's passing spread.

Yankees Club President, Randy Levine, released the following statement:

McCann and Ellsbury are fine, often-injured, broken-down players in the latter parts of their careers, but there is still a chance they might play in a few dozen games next season. Nelson Mandela's blood pressure reading of 0/0 guarantees he won't be active this year at all for us. Last year, players like Alex Rodriguez, Curtis Granderson, Andy Pettitte, and Mariano Rivera came off the DL and provided clutch performances down the stretch. That is not Yankee baseball. In addition, we had Robinson Cano play in 160 of our 162 games. To Yankee fans all over the world, as far as Rodriguez, Granderson, Pettitte, Rivera, and Granderson are concerned, I can proudly say, "problem solved."

This afternoon, the team is poised to introduce Mandela's lifeless body at a press conference at Ruggio's Funeral Home on Arthur Avenue in the Bronx.

December 9, 2013

You can no more level income inequality among the masses than you can level the batting average inequalities among a baseball team.

December 19, 2013 (On A & E's Duck Dynasty Fiasco)

A&E Network, in their infinite wisdom, decides to display their intolerance for one man's words because he displayed his intolerance for another group's actions. A&E is being intentionally ironic, you say? Extremely doubtful because they don't know the meaning of the word. Phil Robertson's words may have come right out of the Koran for all intents and purposes. If a Muslim on the A&E network uttered those exact words, they would have been dead silent.

December 29, 2013

Socialism is the only school of thought in history whose supporters continuously ask you to judge it on its theory instead of its practice.

2014

January 12, 2014

US News & World Report story attributes 5,612 suicides in 2013 to the fact that Joe Flacco has a Super Bowl ring.

January 28, 2014 (SOTU)

(On BO's "If I Had a Son," Trayvon Martin References)

What's the over-under on how many references BO will make to his imaginary son?

Rep. Sheila Jackson, "I must be in the front row."

As usual, Boehner looks like he borrowed George Hamilton's old tanning bed.

Talk about the labor force participation rate, why don't you? That's the actual jobs number, and it's at its lowest point since December 1978.

I'm fairly certain Biden has no idea where he is, and Tan Mom doesn't know when to applaud.

Yes, because 99 weeks of unemployment isn't long enough. Everyone knows that 127 weeks is the magic number for people to find a job.

Why does Dr. Jill Biden always dress as a visiting judge on the 1980s show *Star Search*?

I'm pretty sure whatever Biden is suffering from is considered a pre-existing condition.

Why don't you tell them, BO, how many people have had their policies canceled?

Raise the minimum wage, close Guantanamo! Hey, he's doing all his greatest hits.

Awkward shot catching a bored Jason Collins holding up a Playgirl Centerfold.

January 31, 2014

How long before Mary Jo Buttafuoco and Amy Fisher start to appear together at conventions and card shows signing autographs akin to Ralph Branca and Bobby Thompson? They'll call the convention, "The Shot Heard Round Nassau County."

February 2, 2014

It should be noted that Queen Latifah is not actually royalty.

Does anyone know if the East Rutherford mayor endorsed Christie or not? Fox wants to do a traffic update.

Obama uses Executive Order to give Denver 29 points in his "Equal Score" Act.

February 7, 2014

There aren't many things I don't understand, but my Verizon bill is one of them.

February 8, 2014

A central bank issuing currency is a greater menace to the liberties of the people than a standing militia." (Thomas Jefferson, although the quote is sometimes erroneously credited to Damon Wayans.)

February 9, 2014

I thought the celebration of the Beatles' 50th anniversary on Sullivan was great, except having to see Yoko.

February 11, 2014 (On Passing of the Former Child Star)

An Oval Office-ordered predator drone attack killed Shirley Temple.

February 15, 2014

Although I'm well acquainted with the current economics of "stagflation," it does not seem requisite that a beggar should ask if I can spare a hundred-dollars. My sincerest apologies for not being able to control my burst of laughter in the unfortunate fellow's face.

February 16, 2014

Despite Retirement, Jeter Vows, "Hooking-up will not end"

In a hastily called press conference at Tampa's George M. Steinbrenner Field on Sunday, New York Yankees shortstop and surefire first-ballot Hall-Of-Famer, Derek Jeter, announced to an assembled group of reporters, teammates, team GM Brian Cashman and manager Joe Girardi that although 2014 will be his last season on the field, he has no plans to retire in the bedroom.

In a prepared statement, the 13-time All-Star, whose voice quivered at times with the giddy excitement of a pubescent boy, read:

> To the Steinbrenners, my family and friends, and to the greatest fans in the world, the New York Yankee fans, although earlier this week I announced my retirement from playing baseball after this season, I, today, make a promise to all the hot, young, tail out there, that my days of scoring with you are not nearly done. Don't believe me? Did it end for Bernie Williams after he played his last game in 2006? Those of us who attended *Maxim's* Hot 100 afterparty in 2008 know the answer to that question. And it didn't end for Jorge Posada after the 2011 season. We partied for three days with the girls of *Squish Magazine* at a Miami hotel last season during one of my many stints on the DL.

Jeter's love interests read like a who's who of Hollywood. He has dated Mariah Carey, Jordana Brewster, Vanessa Minnillo, Jessica Alba, Scarlett Johansson, Adriana Lima, Jessica Biel, Minka Kelly, Hannah Davis, Lara Dutta, Rachel Uchitel, Joy Enriquez, Vida Guerra, and Alyssa Milano. But it appears his biggest off-the-field accomplishments may still lie ahead.

> On the field, I have accomplished all my dreams. I've wanted to play shortstop for the New York Yankees since I was a little kid. And what a ride it's been. From winning the Rookie of The Year award and World

Series in '96 to beating our cross-town rivals, the Mets in The Subway Series in 2000, to closing out the old stadium and opening the new one with another title in 2009, the last with "The Core Four." Then there were the twins in Anaheim, the Waffle House waitress in Atlanta, the PR intern in Baltimore, the hostess in Minneapolis, the barista in Seattle, the acrobat in Cleveland, the flight attendants in Kansas City, the entire Hooters staff in Tampa, and the wicked, hot Olive Garden server in Boston, and our interleague games in San Francisco. Oh, don't get me started on San Fran. Tony Bennett may have left his heart there, but I left a nice, big…

Jeter stopped short as his agent and good friend, Casey Close, hit his shoulder. He continued:

It seems just like yesterday I was a skinny, high school prospect hustling hand-jobs from cherubic-faced farm girls in Kalamazoo. How time flies. Yet, I feel that my greatest feats are still ahead of me. I will be around. The Steinbrenners have graciously invited me to come back to spring training next year, and I've accepted. I will be a 'roving instructor,' [the member of the 3,000-hit club said with a wink and a wry smile while using air quotes when stressing the word "roving."] and I can't wait for Old-Timers Day, which I plan to turn into my annual, mid-summer hookup fest in the Bronx.

The Bronx Bombers open the Grapefruit Season with a game against the varsity of The Florida State Seminoles on February 25.

February 22, 2014

So, the frontrunner for the Democratic nominee for president in 2016 is a woman who will be 69 at that point, has uncontrolled blood pressure, suffers fainting spells, has had a blood clot in a vein between her "brain" and her skull, and is most likely suffering from advanced cardiovascular disease. Just out of curiosity, who the hell is polling second?

March 2, 2014 (On the Oscars)

Obama's "red line" to Russia is now "red carpet" at Oscars, and he really means it "this time."

How many more chances will that kid get to be nominated for an Oscar for playing a pirate from his native Somali? #thisisaonceinalifetimechance

Obama set to impose a 2.5 percent excise tax on Dallas Buyer's Club.

Did Penelope Cruz just say, "And the escargot?"

Really, Hollywood? Thanks for that raucous applause when McConaughey wished to thank God. I'm not surprised, but you could have at least "acted" just to please him a bit. You'll never pray in this town again, Mathew McConaughey.

March 7, 2014

Someone needs to tell BO that he is the president of the entire US, all 310 million-plus people. He's not the president of just the one million Americans who don't have health insurance or the 1.6 million who make minimum wage.

March 7, 2014 (On Malaysian Airlines Flight 370)

How the hell do you lose a jet airliner?

March 11, 2014 (On BO's Never-ending Appearances at Beneath the Level of the Office Venues)

Just when we think our brainless leader can't go any lower, he appears on a website called <u>Funny or Die.</u> Seriously? What's next? Will he pitch his failed healthcare plan on a community access show in Northern Virginia?

March 15, 2014

"Those who will sacrifice taste for a bit of calorie-reduction deserve neither."
—Thomas Jefferson

March 29, 2014

Final four for Wisconsin baby. Congrats fellow, Badgers!

March 30, 2014

Today, I am a proud alum of the University of Kaminsky!

April 5, 2014

Every 15 years or so, a new *Godzilla* movie comes out, and I'm not buying it. If a giant lizard could truly kill that many NYC Liberals, the Koch brothers would have thought of it years ago.

April 10, 2014

The following quotes are erroneously credited to Marilyn Monroe but were actually said by Reverend Jeremiah Wright.

"I don't know who invented high heels, but all women owe him a lot."

"A career is wonderful, but you can't curl up with it on a cold night."

"No one ever told me I was pretty when I was a little girl. All little girls should be told they're pretty, even if they aren't."

"What do I wear in bed? Why, Chanel No. 5, of course."

April 16, 2014 (Jackie Robinson Day)

Yesterday and today, we remember a great American, Jackie Robinson. I love him for many reasons, not just because he was a Conservative. He was a guy who showed tremendous courage and faced real hatred and constant death threats. He had to endure racial epithets shouted at him everywhere he went, and not just from southern Dixiecrats. I'm talking about real racism here, not the synthetic kind of today espoused by some wack job MSNBC talking head about how America is still a prejudiced country because Obama won his second term by a smaller margin than his first. We've come a long way, baby.

April 30, 2014 (On Donald Sterling Racism Controversy)

Whoever was behind the alacrity in delivering Donald Sterling his fate in three days should be hired to hightail the Benghazi investigation a year and a half later. But American priorities I suppose. "Nobody ever went broke underestimating the intelligence of the American public." — H.L. Mencken

May 25, 2014

If anyone can dispute my facts, let me know, but this is weird.

The mass shooting that just took place near Santa Barbara was the work of a psychopath who was the son of a *Hunger Games* director. *Hunger Games* is a movie about kids killing others.

The author of *Hunger Games* is Suzanne Collins. She has lived in Sandy Hook, CT, for years with her family. In 2012, the elementary school shootings happened there in Sandy Hook. Sandy Hook was also ground zero for Hurricane Sandy.

Before that, in the movie *Batman Rises*, a map with the words "Sandy Hook" written in pencil is shown. The mass shooting at the Aurora, Colorado theater occurred during a midnight showing of *Batman Rises*.

May 28, 2014 (On Revelation by Robert DeNiro that his Dad was Gay)

What? DeNiro's father was gay? I totally want *A Bronx Tale* redone with Calogero's father telling him these are the best seats he could get him to the Ice-Capades.

Breaking News: Robert DeNiro Sr. was posthumously drafted by the St. Louis Rams.

June 2, 2014

V Stiviano was allegedly severely beaten in NYC Question: How can you tell?

June 16, 2014

Although I'm no soccer fan, I always appreciate the World Cup for no other reason than it's one of the few times Liberals root for America.

July 11, 2014 (On LBJ leaving Miami)

I will not seek, nor accept, the nomination for another four-year term in Miami." — LBJ

July 13, 2014 (On the World Cup)

Congrats to Germany, who gets to visit all the hiding Nazis in South America.

July 17, 2014

Another Malaysia Airlines tragedy. God help them!

(On #lostplane renaissance)

I can sense CNN's ratings about to go back up.

August 1, 2014

Yay! Get your tix now. Ebola is coming to Atlanta.

August 5, 2014

Obama to use Executive Order to grant amnesty to Ebola Virus. The president said, "I've got a pen, and I've got a phone."

August 11, 2014

Robin Williams is dead, and Joy Behar is alive. Life is not fair.

August 22, 2014 (On an Ice Bucket Challenge Parody)

I nominate Steve Hantman, Brett Ladendorf, Erik Rasmussen, and Peter Jacobson to do the Billy Joel Challenge. You have 24 hours to drive your car through the front window of a Long Island family's home or write a check for $1,000 to the "Ol' Piano Man's Lounge" in Montauk.

August 30, 2014

Michael Sam was cut by the Rams but immediately signed by the Bravo Network.

September 25, 2014 (On Bob Costas Always Interjecting Politics into his Play-By-Play)

Jeet's last game at home and I have to listen to Costas call it. Hey Bob, try to refrain from any NRA, pro-choice or domestic violence rants, OK?

Captain Clutch! #farewellcaptain

Sabathia throws out back, picking up Jeter. Transferred to 6000-day DL.

September 27, 2014

So, Romney wants to run in 2016? Do any of you remember when his son said after the 2012 election that his dad didn't really want to be president? Think of how insulting that was to the thousands of campaign volunteers who worked tirelessly without pay to fight for him? To give their all for a man who, in the end, didn't "want to be president." Really? And the American people will fall for it again, you think?

September 30, 2014

I just visited the White House on a tour and got lost and stumbled into the upstairs master bedroom where I came upon Michelle shaving her mustache. I was screaming for five minutes before a Secret Service agent came to my rescue and mercifully extricated me from that situation.

September 30, 2014 (On Celeb Driving Mishaps)

Uber set to hire Billy Joel and Michael Phelps

October 1, 2014

Liberals have always thought with their hearts and not their brains. Now, it appears both organs have been nullified.

October 14, 2014

Obama's Presidency = The Far Less Attractive Rob Lowe

October 16, 2014

Erin Andrews deserves her job as much as the janitorial crew at Dallas Presbyterian Hospital.

November 5, 2014 (On Midterms)

I don't always watch whiny, liberals cry into their lattes, but when I do, it's on PMSNBC on election night. Maryland and Massachusetts both have GOP governors. Wow!

November 24, 2014 (On Ferguson)

My guess is they won't indict Officer Wilson for the shooting of Michael "The Gentle Giant" Brown.

November 24, 2014 (On Ferguson Riots)

Perfect split-screen on Fox. As BO says, "Change will not be made by vandalizing property," the screen on the left shows the agitators attacking a police car. Look at all these geniuses in Ferguson. Let's destroy our neighborhood, riot, and loot, shall we? Just spectacular.

Congratulations to BO, Holder, the Reverends Al, and Jesse for setting back race relations a hundred years in this country.

Will Cigar Aficionado scrap plans to feature the "Gentle Giant" Michael Brown discussing his favorite Swisher Sweet in next month's issue?

November 25, 2014

MSNBC has just hired every Ferguson rioter.

Please join me, Reverend George, tonight in Ferguson, MO, as we protest the St. Louis County DA's unfortunate decision not to prosecute several eyewitnesses who perjured themselves during grand jury testimony in an attempt to make Officer Wilson look guilty. I'll be in my usual tracksuit and medallions.

2015

January 3, 2015

Obama has the unique presidential opportunity to have all six years of his miserable, deplorable commander-in-chief record erased by ordering one predator drone strike against Russell Brand. #killrussellnow

January 3, 2015

Opening Day is only three months away, which means the New York Yankees have only 94 days to fill the Disabled List.

January 7, 2015 (On the Charlie Hebdo Massacre)

Hearts and prayers to my brothers and sisters in satire in Paris.

January 20, 2015 (SOTU)

After tonight, there's only one more BO State of the Union. Thank God!

Boehner is finally the same color as the red stripes on Old Glory behind him.

The energy secretary looks like the crazy music teacher from middle school who taught in a classroom by the boiler room.

If the economy is such a success, how can a two-income family be a necessity?

When will you go on paid sick leave, BO?

I bet Rep. Sheila Jackson Lee thinks Bookman on *Good Times* was a hoot.

I thought you were going to close Gitmo six years ago, BO?

March 10, 2015 (On Hillary's server press conference)

Bill Clinton on today's presser: "Server? I don't even know her."

Does she really not know you can't put two mail accounts on one phone? She's either lying or too stupid to be a wireless store employee, let alone president.

April 3, 2015

To show our contempt for those who discriminate, we will discriminate against them.

If the Left still doesn't get the irony, allow me to paraphrase and allude to one of their favorite slogans during wartime: "Why do we kill people who kill people to show killing people is wrong?"

April 4, 2015 (On My Badgers in the Final Four)

Look, I really don't care if you guys are rooting for Wisconsin or Kentucky but let's all just remember that Kentucky still has segregated lunch counters.

April 14, 2015 (On Hillary Burrito Gate)

In other news, old lady goes unnoticed at Chipotle.

Congrats, Libs. You've seen the future, and it's White, geriatric multi-millionaires.

Where's "Scary" Reid yelling to see this prehistoric relic's tax returns?

April 23, 2015

A five-year joint study conducted by the Department of Homeland Security and FBI concludes that 85 percent of all US violence is a result of Carlos Gomez being hit by pitch.

April 25, 2015

What do you think will hurt Bruce Jenner more in Hollywood, his sex change, or coming out as a Republican?

April 26, 2015

Town Still Recovering from Lisa Kudrow Visit

One month ago, Wellington, KS was struck by a deadly visit from actress Lisa Kudrow that destroyed homes and leveled businesses. In the aftermath of the former *Friends* star's appearance, this little town, with a population of 8,172, has struggled to rebuild.

Lifelong Wellington resident and former Mayor Jim Buckner remembers exactly where he was when Kudrow first struck.

"I was having coffee in Penny's Diner when the whistles went off. We barely had time to get to the safe room in the schoolhouse before she got through 'Smelly Cat.'"

But not everyone was as lucky. 67-year-old Kaye Browner and her sister, 75-year-old Julie Garson, were killed just minutes into the 51-year-old Emmy winner's story about dating Conan O'Brien in college. Rebecca Dysart, a receptionist at a dental clinic and mother of four, lost her home and all her belongings when Kudrow fumed about David Schwimmer's inability to pull off a spit-take.

Trisha Lamont, owner of Trish's Cakes, a bakery in what was once considered downtown Wellington, lamented, "The sad part is the town was just starting to recover from Alfonso Ribeiro's touchdown here in 2011. Now we must rebuild again. It's still just too much," she sobbed before collapsing into the arms of a Red Cross volunteer.

But other residents are more hopeful.

"Just because *The Comeback* goes on a nine-year hiatus doesn't mean Wellington has to as well," advised Jim LaGrande, a member of the city council. His words are taking effect as construction on a new hospital, the Presbyterian Church, and several businesses along Main Street flattened during Kudrow's *Analyze That* tour are now underway.

"Someday, we will have to explain to our children what happened here; those too young to comprehend it now," advised Police Chief Larry MacMurray. "It will take a lot of strength, courage, and a DVD of *Michele and Romy's High School Reunion*, but we will explain, and we will get through this."

At press time, residents are bracing for the worst as reports of a Joyce DeWitt sighting 150 miles southeast in Tulsa are pouring in.

May 1, 2015

In Emotional Farewell, Jeter, and Pettitte Remove Sabathia from Life Support

New York —In an unexpected move, Yankee manager Joe Girardi sent franchise legends Derek Jeter and Andy Pettitte to the mound to remove pitcher CC Sabathia from life support during yesterday's matchup between the Bronx Bombers and their archrival, the Boston Red Sox at Yankee Stadium.

"It's something we talked about in the clubhouse before the game in case he got in trouble early," Girardi admitted to a crowd of reporters and orderlies in his office shortly after the 24-0 Boston victory. "This is the way CC would have wanted to go out, with dignity."

With Boston already ahead 17-0 on a grand slam from David Ortiz and Hanley Ramirez due up next in the top of the second, Girardi, with permission from Sabathia's family, decided to pull the plug on the hefty southpaw. However, in a move usually reserved for managers, pitching coaches, or attending physicians, Girardi had Yankee greats Jeter and Pettitte walk out of the first base side home dugout to take the 2007 American League Cy Young award winner off the ventilator. Once Pettitte handed the lineup card and "Do Not Resuscitate" form to Umpire Crew Chief John Hirschbeck, it was all but a formality. Sabathia's pitching line and his life were over. A few seconds later, the Yankees team captain undid the tracheostomy tube with his left hand, and in classic Jeter fashion, fist pumped with his right. There was barely a dry eye among the sell-out crowd of 50,291 fans.

Jeter and Pettitte then wheeled the 2009 ALCS MVP's lifeless body off the mound to Notorious BIG's "Big Poppa" and a standing ovation from the Bronx faithful to make way for reliever Chris Martin, who will someday be the answer to a trivia question.

"CC just didn't have command of his fastball tonight or a living will, so it was the right move," defended a visibly tired Girardi.

Yet, the pitching decision was not without doubters and questioned by the Twitterverse, including Peter Gammons and the Terri Schiavo Foundation.

"I thought about it long and hard," conceded Girardi. "Moving CC to the bullpen was unlikely considering the job those guys have done so far this season. For CC to continue living, we'd have to send another lefty down to Scranton, and Chase Shreven is out of options. What would you do?" the World Series-winning manager asked rhetorically.

"We checked with MLB and the organ donor association and followed all the proper protocol," added Yankee General Manager Brian Cashman. "So, kids, if you want to be like CC, be an organ donor."

In other news, first baseman Mark Texeira won AL Player of the Week honors with his recent offensive tear.

May 1, 2015

Los Angeles—Donald Sterling Looking to Purchase MLB Team, Wants to Un-retire Jackie Robinson's # 42. "Enough of this bullshit."

May 13, 2015 (On Yankee Ace's injury)

Tanaka feels good after the second bullpen session; he will be injected with Bartolo Colon on Friday.

May 16, 2015

Hi, I'm Hillary Clinton, candidate for president of the United States. Recently, my husband Bill and I earned over $25 million for speeches. Today I'd like to talk to you about income inequality in America.

May 16, 2015

Hi, I'm Hillary Clinton, candidate for president of the United States. My husband Bill has been accused of rape, sexual assault, or misconduct against women at least 11 times in his life. I was Secretary of State for four years for an administration that paid its female employees 13 percent less than their male counterparts. Today I want to talk to you about the GOP's war on women.

May 22, 2015

There is a middle-aged man in Starbucks wearing a Jon Secada T-shirt. The only thing more embarrassing in the world than that would be if you were actually Jon Secada.

For the 16th year in a row, Reginald Vel Johnson tops the FBI's list of Ten Most Wanted Fugitives.

May 23, 2015

Yankees Set to Retire Kevin Youkilis' Number on Sunday

New York — In a move hailed as long overdue by many baseball aficiona-dos, the New York Yankees will retire Kevin Youkilis' number 36 during a pre-game ceremony in the Bronx before tomorrow's game with the Texas Rangers.

"Youk," as he was affectionately known in Boston during his produc-tive years, had a three-and-a-half-month tenure with the Yankees during their fabled 2013 season. He posted a.219 batting average, two home runs, and eight RBIs. He was paid a million dollars for each run he scored (12) in a total of 28 games before being lost for the season on June 14th.

On Sunday, Youkilis will take his rightful place in Monument Park behind the centerfield wall in Yankee Stadium alongside such fellow Yankee legends as Babe Ruth, Lou Gehrig, Joe DiMaggio, Yogi Berra, and Mickey Mantle. In addition to his retired jersey, he will have a plaque with the inscription, "Kevin Youkilis, 2013-2013. Once got hit by pitch in late sea-son spring training intra-squad game to move Corban Joseph into scor-ing position."

According to the Yankees Public Relations office, Youkilis will address the Bronx faithful one last time, no doubt to the same cheers of "You-Kill-Us!" that he heard sandwiched between his three stints on the Disabled List.

In true Yankee fashion, the team plans to bring back many of Youkilis' former Bronx Bomber iconic teammates, including Luis Cruz, Jayson Nix, Zoilo Almonte, Cesar Cabral, Brent Lilibridge, Brennan Boesch, and Reid Brignac. They'll flank the owner of a.343 Yankee career Slugging Percentage as he and the expected sell-out crowd watch highlights of his Yankee career on the diamond vision in center field which will include the time he waved Melky Mesa home from third on a wild pitch, his batting practice line-drive off the left field wall in Cleveland against Yankees coach Tony Pena and his signing with the Tohoku Rakuten Golden Eagles of the Japanese Nippon Professional Baseball Pacific League. In other news, the Yankees have announced that the September 8 game against the Minnesota Twins will be Garrett Jones Bobblehead Night.

June 1, 2015

I'm not saying that Sen. Lindsey Graham is gay. I'm just saying it's strange he decided to announce his candidacy for president next to the Chippendale's male revue.

June 10, 2015

Fox News Alert — Republican presidential candidate Sen. Lindsey Graham set to debate former Democratic US Rep. Barney Frank on immigration, the future of Obamacare, and *Magic Mike XXL*.

June 11, 2015 (On NY Fugitives)

Senator Lindsey Graham agrees to join manhunt in NY State.

June 15, 2015 (On the Rachel Dolezal fiasco)

Ahh! Having a couple of cold ones and reminiscing about all the occasions my parents outed me as a Caucasian. Good times.

June 25, 2015

The Supreme Court's unfortunate decision regarding exchanges and subsidies for the ACA once again proves that the US government has, in a short time, descended from a constitutional republic to a faux democracy to judicial tyranny. If the exact text of the law doesn't matter and can be ignored by activist judges with agendas, then SCOTUS is no more worthy of serious jurisprudence than top courts of countries like South Africa, whose justices create policy instead of upholding the Constitution.

(On Obama's use of the N-word on Marc Maron podcast)

Hey BO, try not to use the N-Word again when you no doubt gloat over today's ruling at your presser.

June 27, 2015

I, for one, am not at all surprised by Justice Kennedy's majority opinion in yesterday's landmark Supreme Court case regarding same sex marriage. A close inspection of his prior rulings shed some insight into how he might adjudicate.

In Franklin vs. the US, he wrote that one does have the right to "yell 'Fire Island' in a crowded porn theater." 2012 saw the year where Kennedy found US Solicitor Donald B. Verrilli Jr. "guilty of being adorable." Last, in the watershed Andy Cohen v. Queen Bee Salon & Spa, he determined that "separate but equally fabulous spas are inherently, unequally fabulous." Yesterday, Kennedy underscored his long-held beliefs when he paused from reading his opinion to ask Chief Justice Roberts if he could "search his briefs and look for his subpoena" if you know what I mean."

July 5, 2015 (On Women's World Cup)

It's a day like today which makes me proud to live in a country that pretends it cares about soccer.

Prediction on future SCOTUS decision circa 2018. Chief Justice Roberts saves SoloCare's.

Individual Mandate for Americans to purchase soccer tickets by declaring it a "tax" and not a penalty.

July 9, 2015 (On Kate Steinle Shooting)

Recent quotes regarding Francisco Sanchez:

"He's not an illegal alien; he's an undocumented marksman." — Hillary Clinton

"If I had a gardener, he would look like Francisco Sanchez." — Barack Obama

July 13, 2015

Mr. Belvedere Fans to Gather Outside UN in Call for Climate Change Policy Reform: Memories of Groundbreaking Show Revived

New York — On what would have been actor Christopher Hewitt's 94th birthday, tens of thousands of fans of his hit 1980s sitcom, *Mr. Belvedere,* will assemble outside the UN on August 3rd to protest in favor of global action to combat climate change.

Mr. Belvedere tackled social and geopolitical themes in many of its episodes, which paved the way for progressive ideas and policies to be enacted in our society. Bryan Moore of Madison, WI, who is helping to organize the rally, said, "We believe that even today, a quarter of a century after the second and final tragic cancelation of a show detailing the slapstick hijinks of an English butler and a dysfunctional suburban Pittsburgh family, that there is no stronger force for the good of our environment than the spirit of one Christopher Hewitt."

"The show explored acute issues of racism, sexism, the environment, and inequitable economic policies years before they were widely discussed or considered to be in vogue and socially palatable," said TV critic Matt Eindt. "Who was dealing with transgender equality, CO_2 emissions, unequal pay for women, and the removal of the Confederate Flag in the 1980s?" "*Mr. Belvedere,* that's who," Eindt explained.

Admirers of the show will never forget the shocking yet iconic episode in which Owens family patriarch George, played by baseballer turned broadcaster turned actor Bob Eucker, is killed in an apartheid protest in Johannesburg shortly after unwittingly helping son Wesley win a spelling bee against the class nerd.

In another episode, "Just Desserts," which aired on February 25, 1988, and is still the second most-watched television program in history, according to Nielsen, Mr. Belvedere needs extra cash and is hired to cater a gay wedding. George assumes the cake in the fridge belongs to the family and mistakenly eats it. With time running out, Mr. Belvedere is forced to hire a bakery to replace the cake but is denied due to their anti-gay stance. The wedding eventually gets canceled, leading to the demise of the gay couple (played convincingly by Harvey Fierstein and Boy George O' Dowd) and their double suicide, but not before a good old-fashioned pie fight breaks out.

"I remember watching that night," recalls Ellen DeGeneres. "While Morgan Fairchild was taking a lemon meringue pie to the face, the LGBT community was taking one more step toward equality."

"That episode takes on a lot," writes Jorgensen Stierem, a professor of Communications at UCLA. "Commentary on the real-life pieing of anti-gay activist Anita Bryant, the murder of Harvey Milk and the brilliant spit-take performed by Brice Beckham."

Still, the show was not without its critics. In 2004, in what was initially considered a slam dunk, a House bill dedicated to making Ilene Graf's birthday a federal holiday died a slow death in the US Senate shortly after a 23-hour filibuster from Pennsylvania Republican Senator Rick Santorum.

And in 2012, efforts to have Rob Stone's likeness added to Mt. Rushmore were dashed when even Liberal Congressman Barney Frank of Massachusetts wondered aloud about the appropriateness of putting the Dallas-born actor's face next to those of our most revered presidents. Apparently, Frank was unmoved by the Twitter campaign #getstoneonthestone.

Bill Donaghue of the Catholic League said, "The show was nothing more than another Liberal Hollywood export using slapstick humor to hide the fact that it was a mouthpiece for the Far-left secular progressive agenda, including their incorrect stance that climate change is real and man-made." Donaghue cited the episode "Beach Pittsburgh USA" as an example. The episode revolves around Brice Beckham's character, Wesley T. Owens, the family's youngest son. Wesley steals Belvedere's cherished diary and reads it aloud to the family. It's also the first time we learn Belvedere's first name, much to Wesley's amusement, who opines, "Lynn? That's a girl's name!"

The big revelation is that Mr. Belvedere has written extensively on the surge of CO_2 emissions warming the earth's temperatures.

"Hey Belvedere, you don't really believe any of that crap that warmer temperatures will melt the polar ice caps and raise sea levels, do ya'?" George Owens responds. "Hey kids, ol' Belvedere here is stupid enough to believe that one day Pittsburgh will be oceanfront property."

Daughter Heather Owens (Tracy Wells) and Wesley perk up.

"A beach here in Pittsburgh? Cool." exclaims Wesley.

Belvedere then dumps a tub of ice water over the trio, "How cool was that, Wesley?"

Donaghue's belief put him at odds with his church leader, noted global climatologist Pope Francis, who believes climate change is man-made. Moore plans on quoting extensively from that episode when addressing the crowd on August 3rd.

"The Owens family always learned great lessons from that gifted English butler, and I'm hoping that UN Secretary-General Ban Ki-moon will be equally moved."

July 17, 2015 (On being back in my home state of New Jersey)

I just got off the plane to an Italian woman berating her husband in public. It's good to be home.

July 23, 2015

Why aren't we implementing a minimum skill instead of a minimum wage?

August 26, 2015 (On Virginia News On-Air Murders)

Today's horrible news out of Virginia is reminiscent of the Christine Chubbuck story from 1974, but hers was a live suicide in front of only 1,000 viewers, or so, that took place in the pre-VCR days. As I understand it, the only tape of Chubbuck's suicide was from the station, who turned it over to the police as evidence. The tape was later given to her family, who destroyed it.

October 13, 2015 (On Baseball and Dem Debate)

Flipping between Mets game and debate and for nearly 30 seconds confused Hillary Clinton for Bartolo Colon.

Hillary's Wall Street/Banking Plan "Too Big to Nail."

Which Farrelly Brothers Comedy was Lincoln Chaffee in?

Secretary Clinton, what will be the first thing you will do Day One as an inmate?

Loved Bernie Sanders on *Curb Your Enthusiasm*.

October 20, 2015 (On Playoff baseball on TBS)

I would like to thank TBS for providing closed-captioned translations of Pedro Martinez's commentary.

October 27, 2015

Make-A-Wish Foundation grants dying boy's request to see Joe Girardi fired.

November 1, 2015 (On World Series Champion KC Royals)

I'm sure Girardi is completely befuddled by a team like KC that steals bases and manufactures runs-the way the game is supposed to be played.

November 14, 2015 (On Paris Terrorist Attacks)

There are two kinds of people in the world: (1) those whose first reaction to the Paris tragedy is to be saddened by what happened, and whose sympathies lie with the dead and injured; and (2) those whose first reaction to the Paris tragedy is to say, "Well, it's important to remember that "these violent perpe-trators" are not an accurate representation of Islam and whose sympathies lie at the altar of political correctness. If your natural reaction is the first, then your head is in the right place. If it's the second, you need to re-evaluate where life went wrong for you.

December 8, 2015

Even though he was assassinated 35 years ago today, let us remember John Lennon's life and not his death.

"Hey, that's The Dakota, that's where John Lennon died." — *Gawker*

"No, that's where John Lennon lived." — Bob Gruen, Lennon photographer, and close friend

December 31, 2015 (NYE Flashback Apparently)

I just asked everyone at the party to put on Dick Clark for the countdown. #gettingold #happynewyear

2016

February 1, 2016 (On the Dem Candidates' Dismal Support)

Martin O' Malley's supporters advised by the campaign staff chief not to call him "Dad" in public.

February 7, 2016 (On Super Bowl and Peyton's Last Game)

"What a way to ride off in the sunset in my final NFL game. My only regret is that America at halftime had to pretend that Beyoncé is a legitimate musical talent." (Peyton Manning)

February 10, 2016

There's been a ton of posts about Beyoncé and her shameful halftime performance. But I will say this; Beyoncé is just a virus. For a virus to survive, it must attach itself to a host cell. In this instance, that host cell is the NFL.

February 23, 2016 (On CNN Dem Town Hall)

The sexual tension between Chris Cuomo and Hillary Clinton is unmistakable.

Did I just hear that right? A young African American woman told Hillary she has started wearing her hair naturally and is essentially afraid of the potential consequences? Gotta love the fake, manufactured questions the DNC and CNN gave to audience members to see whether Bernie or Hillary will pander more to Black voters.

February 24, 2016 (On Obama's Plan to Congress to Close Guantanamo Bay Prison)

I know people are up in arms over Gitmo today. All I know is not to feed it after midnight or get water on it.

February 25, 2016 (On Republican Debate)

Really, Hugh? Asking Rubio to release his tax returns is like asking George Will to detail his sexual escapades.

March 3, 2016

Will Hillary be getting a running mate or cellmate?

March 8, 2016

I'm digging in for a night of election coverage with Bret Baier and Nicole Brown Simpson.

The Democratic primaries and caucuses are almost as big a fraud as Hillary. Coin tosses, corrupt pledged super delegate rules, and the like. I can't believe Bernie the Bolshevik's supporters aren't more up in their unworked arms.

March 15, 2016

What is up with Hillary's persistent cough?

His slogan is just as underwhelming as he is: "Kasich Works."

Kasich is the kind of guy that brags about getting some from his wife.

Fox News is in a tizzy over big Trump night. Delusional Boss Hog says Kasich will do well in upcoming Northeast states.

In his spare time, Kasich coaches the Washington Generals

So Ancestry.com will give you a 10 percent discount on a St. Patty's Day DNA test to see if you're Irish. Wouldn't a sobriety test be more effective?

March 29, 2016 (On Republican Debate)

That sound you hear is ten million people changing the channel now that Kasich is on.

I can't decide if Kasich played a neighbor in "The Monsters Are Due on Maple Street" or if he was the agent who used the "Ben Franklin close" on me after I initially balked at his offer of purchasing supplemental life insurance.

Kasich brags about endorsement from the *Waukesha Freeman* and Willy Aames.

Kasich's sincerity smacks square between Robert Shapiro and that capsized Italian cruise ship captain guy.

April 26, 2016

Just out of curiosity, who the hell lost to Kasich for Governor of Ohio?

The Secret Service nickname for him: "Kasich."

April 27, 2016

Lyin' Carly! She puts the HP manual down, and she starts lyin'.

May 3, 2016

When the primaries are done, Donald Trump is predicted by analysts to have garnered more than 12 million votes. This would be a record number of votes for a Republican primary candidate, eclipsing George W. Bush's total in 2000. Even more remarkably, Trump did it in a year where he defeated 16 other Republican candidates.

It took "Lyin' Carly" Fiorina years to destroy HP...She did it to the Cruz campaign in just one week.

Ted Cruz to end campaign from Indiana basketball ring.

Rafael Cruz tries to slowly exit stage during son's speech before being stopped by Shaggy and Scooby-Doo.

How bad is Bill Clinton looking forward to having Melania Trump as First Lady? You can already hear the Chappaqua Fire Department's first hose extinguishing Billy's crotch.

Funny how the unscrupulous media has been reporting that Republicans are "for sure" headed to a contested GOP convention. Trump became the presumptive nominee earlier in the primary season than Romney did in 2012.

Only in the United States can a Canadian accused of being an American serial killer drop out of a presidential race on the same day his Cuban father is accused of killing JFK.

May 4, 2016

Breaking News: "Kreepy Kasich" to exit race and return to his home at 1313 Mockingbird Lane.

May 5, 2016 (On Allegiant Air Mishaps)

How bad is Allegiant Air? Fifty percent of their pilots won't let their own families fly on it. Seven injuries from turbulence are hard to do unless you're Balki from *Perfect Strangers*.

May 19, 2016

Today's health tip: If you want to continue living, don't retire from *60 Minutes*. Both Andy Rooney and now Morley Safer died right after leaving the show.

May 24, 2016

Super Bowl returns to Atlanta. Ray Lewis is excited about coming out of retirement for "one more kill."

June 15, 2016 (On Disney Tragedy and Scalia's Passing)

A two-year-old is snatched in front of a crowd by an alligator, dragged to the water, and they schedule an autopsy. A US Supreme Court Justice dies alone under suspicious circumstances on a trip to Texas and no autopsy is conducted.

I say whoever oversaw the Seven Seas Lagoon's Search and Destroy mission that wiped out five gators in a kill-first, ask-questions-later manner, hightail it to the Middle East to dispense some justice Disney-style.

June 23, 2016

Now that the "Stairway to Heaven" lawsuit has been settled, motion to move on to new business from 1972? Do I have a second?

June 24, 2016 (On BREXIT)

Late 2017- Awkward moment when EU runs into Great Britain on a crowded London Street,

    EU: "You look...happy."

    GB: "Thanks, I am!"

EU: "Look...maybe we can get a drink or something sometime?"

GB: "EU, look, it's over."

June 26, 2016

In honor of George Will leaving the Republican Party, let's look back at some of his most memorable quotes:

"Live fast, die young, and leave a beautiful corpse."

"With my first bonus check, I spent most of it on booze and broads, the rest I just wasted."

"Is sex dirty? Only when it's being done right."

"I am on a drug. It's called Charlie Sheen. It's not available. If you try it once, you will die. Your face will melt off and your children will weep over your exploded body."

July 26, 2016 (On DNC and Bill Discussing Hillary)

Bill, you met a girl in 1971? Would you care to be more specific? The only story I wanna hear ol' Bill tell involves the twins from *Hee Haw*.

Chelsea's husband looks like the guy who just sold you a double indemnity plan and doesn't wait until he is out of sight to high-five his manager on the co-travel.

In 2008, it was "Hope and Change." In 2016, it's "Change Maker." If the past eight years were such a success and Hillary was such a big part of that success as Secretary of State, why all the need to make change?

July 27, 2016 (On VP Nominee Kaine speaking)

There it is again, "fair share of taxes." Hey Timmy, people pay their legal share of taxes according to their brackets, not their "fair share," whatever the hell that is.

Obama went on so late that the DNC feared most of their base had already passed out with the needle in their arms.

July 28, 2016

Did Jennifer Granholm just talk about the coal miner in W. Virginia? "Jen, you do realize that Hillary wants to shut down that industry, right?" SMH

Whoever just yelled, "Black Lives Matter" during the moment of silence for the fallen police officers is truly a POS. Stay classy, Dems.

So, from which device does Hillary FaceTime her granddaughter?

Wait, "way too many dreams die in the parking lots of banks?" I guess Hillary would know when she's inside them making millions for a speech.

August 13, 2016 (On A-Rod's Retirement)

Yankee Stadium Security sent to escort A-Rod out of stadium after he cleaned out locker. A-Rod seen exiting building with cardboard box filled with potted plant, family photos, and Louisville Slugger.

August 27, 2016

I'll bet if it was a glory hole in the Castro, Kaepernik would be standing erect.

September 1, 2016

With Trump surging in the recent polls (ahead in some), when will Hillary have him killed and how?

September 7, 2016 (On Hillary's Health Issues)

Whether Hillary is dying of Tuberculosis or heart disease, what difference, at this point, does it make?

September 8, 2016

Everyone is talking about Hillary wearing an earpiece during the interview last night, but no one is concerned about Trump wearing a hairpiece. Bald Lives Matter. #theyllbehelltoupee

September 20, 2016

Another campaign event canceled by Hillary. She does not look good. Can't be in public for very long. Eyes having trouble focusing. Needs help to climb stairs at Temple. Appears to be drugged on airplane on Sunday discussing the bombings. Is it "just" Parkinson's?? Something worse? Where are her loved ones? Why are they letting her continue to go through all of this? OR Is her ambition usurping the advice of her Dr.'s and family?

September 21, 2016 (On Charlotte Riots)

I'm disingenuously upset by a false narrative manufactured by the mainstream media--so let's break shit in Charlotte. Genius! 👍

September 30, 2016

Gary Johnson is the greatest public service announcement against drug use since the "I learned it by watching you, dad" campaign in the 1980s.

Gary Johnson once got stuck for three days on a broken escalator. Gary Johnson makes Biden look like de Tocqueville.

October 4, 2016 (On VP Debate)

Forty million people just said in unison, "Who the hell is Elaine Quijano?!"

Kaine is the high school guidance counselor who always called you by the wrong name.

Somebody at CBS needs to teach Quijano what a follow-up question is. How about getting a hold of the time clock as well?

The 1972 Olympic basketball game between the Soviet Union and USA was better officiated.

I'm ready for Hank Iba to wander onto the stage.

The citizens of Aleppo have no idea who Gary Johnson is.

Tim Kaine is an unhinged sociopath.

If she is just there to read off a paper sheet and not ask any follow-ups or "moderate," then why do we need a moderator?

Pence is writing his rebuttals in pen, whereas Kaine is writing with a Magic Marker as he is not allowed to have sharp objects on his person.

OJ Simpson on Tim Kaine, "Now that guy's fucking nuts!"

October 19, 2016

Remember, folks, Wikileaks is doing the job that a fair and honest media would do. It's a shame we don't have one here in the US.

October 19, 2016

Incredibly, the Democrats have to pay people $1,500 to start violence in Chicago when they do it for free every day. Another example of poor negotiating by the Left.

Hillary has participated in several debates. First when she ran for New York Senator against Rick Lazio in 2000. In 2008, she first ran for president but lost the nomination to BO. In 2016, she ran for the Democratic nomination and now the presidency. Trump has done two debates so far, and he destroyed her. How the hell is a career politician "out-politicianed" by a guy running not to be a politician? Wait, I think I just answered my question.

(On Larry King Sitting Behind Home Plate for Dodger Playoff Games)

More people have watched Larry King on TV the past two nights than in his 25 years on CNN.

October 26, 2016

Another shameful interview by Megyn. She's letting what's left of her journalistic integrity be clouded by her hatred of Trump and his supporters. Or is this another audition tape for one of the three major networks?

October 27, 2016

Sorry all, but I won't be watching "*Sex Talk with Nicole Brown Simpson*" anymore.

October 28, 2016 (On Comey Reopening of the Clinton Investigation)

That loud sound you just heard is the noise of social media exploding.

October 29, 2016

I guess Bill Clinton and Loretta Lynch will just happen to meet again on a tarmac somewhere this week.

Warning: There's an email circulating with subject header: "Nude Pictures of Hillary Clinton." Please do not click the attachment as it is nude pictures of Hillary Clinton.

November 3, 2016

Fifty percent of current Hillary voters were alive the last time the Cubs won the World Series in 1908.

November 8, 2016 (Election Night)

Florida is a nail-biter as it was in 2012. The panhandle part of the state is very Pro-Trump, and many of those votes have yet to be counted as it's in the Central Time Zone and polls closed later.

Dr. Charles Krauthammer's interview with Bill O'Reilly on Fox earlier tonight was shameful and disingenuous. I'm not sure what happened to this man. Dr. Krauthammer, allow **me** to play the role of psychiatrist and analyze **you**. You have allowed your hatred of Trump to cloud your ability for rationale, sanity, and insight. A mistake common for a man who wears much younger clothes than you. In short order, you have descended from being the intellectual head of the GOP to a Never Trumper to an unhinged, foaming at the mouth, talking head whose anger has usurped his cerebral cortex.

Fox News is doubling down on stupid. What election are they watching this evening? Nicole Brown Simpson is once again leading her cadre of idiots into a mental banana-slip face-first into the layman's cake at the "Ignorance Ball." I'm embarrassed. I've turned to CNN as they have been providing more "fair and balanced" coverage thus far.

Ron Johnson wins! No one had that one! Way to go to my old home state of Wisconsin. Feingold can stay retired.

The Electoral College map was just found shot dead with a bullet wound in the back of the head and a suicide note attached.

CNN has mysteriously stopped calling states that Fox called an hour ago. LOL!

What the hell is Dana Perino talking about on Fox? "Paul Ryan got Wisconsin for Trump?" Does she not know he decided to focus on the House races and purposely told Trump he was on his own?

Rachel Maddow hasn't been this upset since Cagney and Lacey got canceled.

I'm not surprised that PMSNBC still hasn't called so many states for Trump that were announced hours ago on Fox, as they still haven't called Ohio for Bush in 2004.

November 9, 2016

Thank you, Julian Assange, for doing the job our media refuses.

Clinton won't concede tonight as she went to bed hours ago.

Karl Rove's epic meltdown was classic! Say goodbye to the establishment RINO Republican Party. Don't let the door hit you in your bloated, lazy derrieres.

AP and *NY Times* call Pennsylvania for Trump, putting him over 270! Congrats, President Trump!

Sending Podesta out as a surrogate for Hillary is kind of a microcosm for her entire campaign-MIA

Clinton Conceded!

This is just a reminder to all who still don't think the media is crooked. Hillary Clinton had to call the election tonight. None of the networks did.

Gotta' love Speaker Ryan's post-election endorsement of Trump. Ryan went on to say he thinks Cubs will win in seven.

November 11, 2016 (On Online Phony Quotes)

"For the life in me I can't explain this, but from the moment I shook hands with this man, I had a feeling he would someday lead this great nation of ours." (Abraham Lincoln on Donald Trump)

November 12, 2016

Hmm, I'm just curious, if Hillary did nothing wrong or illegal in connection to her deleted emails and private server, as we were told repeatedly by the left during the election, why are they clamoring for Obama to pardon her?

November 19, 2016 (On the Timeless and Equally Intimidating Matt Barnes)

Every year Matt Barnes makes the NBA roster means one cell in San Quentin is still available.

November 22, 2016

Trump seemingly letting HRC off the hook reeks of Hanks throwing that German soldier back into rotation in *Saving Private Ryan*. If her health holds up - and that's a big if, she will run again in 2020. I'm just saying, when you can destroy your opponent, do it. Trump would be well-served to heed my advice. Hoping he's just allowing revenge to be a dish best served cold.

December 11, 2016

Anybody remember when a guy named Nate Silver was relevant? I suppose he's back home in Detroit getting ready to handicap Detroit Tiger's games in a few months.

December 13, 2016

Cuisinart just recalled eight million food processors. From where? 1987?

December 20, 2016

Congratulations, Hillary Clinton! You lost an Electoral College vote today in Washington state to someone named Spotted Eagle, which is not a reference to your husband.

December 20, 2016

If you're keeping score at home, let's recap the final Electoral College score: Faith Spotted Eagle-1. Jill Stein-0

2017

January 20, 2017 (On Inauguration of Donald John Trump)

May God Bless our 45th President, Donald J. Trump, and may God Bless the United States of America.

February 9, 2017

In 1913, before they were famous (or more accurately, infamous), Adolf Hitler, Joseph Stalin, Leon Trotsky, Joseph Tito, and Sigmund Freud all lived in Vienna, a few miles apart from each other, and frequented the same coffee houses. My question is, what the hell was in that coffee?

February 18, 2017

Amazing fact number one: The grandchildren of John Tyler, the tenth president of our country, who was born in 1790 are still alive as of February 2017. John Tyler served as POTUS from 1841-1845, that's 20 years before Abraham Lincoln was assassinated.

February 23, 2017

Watching *My 600 lb. Life*. Now I'm starving.

February 26, 2017 (On Oscar Ceremony and mishap)

Half of the Oscars ceremony tonight will be the segment where they honor those who passed away the previous year.

Worst opening monologue ever. I've always said Kimmel is the luckiest no talent comedian since Jimmy Carter. From hack jokes to asking for applause to kill time, to no delivery, this guy makes Carlos Mencia look like Lenny Bruce.

Whether that was scripted or not, who knows? Seems a bit close to the Steve Harvey thing. My guess is it wasn't. The Oscars take themselves too seriously to allow that to happen.

I think Faye Dunaway just jeopardized her chances for *Dunston Checks In, Part Two.*

February 28, 2017 (On Donald J. Trump's first Public Address before a Joint Session of Congress)

So, putting American citizens first again is a line that draws partisan support?

"Radical Islamic Terrorism." Yup, it's a new president.

I think the paid family leave thingy was thrown in there just to see if the Dems were listening at all.

The Dems believe that you can choose any school you want so long as it's a failing, public school with a strong union and tenured non-terminable teachers.

Over 100,000 people were shot and killed during this speech in Chicago.

Stupid, silly Dem protest at the end. Keep it up, Dems. You've lost 1,200 seats in nine years. In another nine years, you will cease to exist as a party.

When did Pelosi die? She has resting in peace bitch face.

(On Dem. Response to Speech)

I'm halfway waiting for Gov. Beshear to don an apron and start sweeping up shop.

March 8, 2017

A-Rod and J-Lo? Oh No. A-New-Lo.

March 20th, 2017

Maybe FBI Director James Comey is an idiot. "The reason I hate the Patriots is that they represent sustained excellence and as a NY Giants fan, this drives me nuts," he said while testifying before Congress today. Perhaps someone should tell Comey that the team he is supposedly a fan of beat Brady and the Patriots in the Super Bowl twice in the past 10 years.

April 14, 2017

CNN set to honor all 36 ISIS members killed by "mother of all bombs" with slow, video montage remembrance of their lives tonight at 8:00 p.m.

May 3, 2017

Amazing that the GOP controls both houses of Congress, all three branches of the federal government, 33 of 50 state governorships, and most of the local government, but the Dems still have the final say on everything.

May 8, 2017

You're in a room with Joe Girardi and North Korean dictator Kim Jong Un. You have a gun with two bullets in it. What do you do? You shoot Girardi twice of course.

May 9, 2017

I think the one thing we can all agree on, Right or Left, is that Comey was an absolute disaster.

May 19, 2017

New Uber option lets drivers cancel their passenger's health insurance after five minutes.

June 14, 2017

Prayers for Rep. Steve Scalise and others wounded in this morning's tragedy.

June 17, 2017 (On Protestors Interrupting Trump Parody Play)

The Right is finally waking up, getting off their collective arses and employing the fighting spirit the Left has for years in this country.

June 20, 2017

Congrats to Karen Handel, who tonight won Georgia's 6th Congressional District seat. Most expensive race in history. Preponderance of her opponent's money came from out of state. SMH!

Once again, the polls were intentionally skewed. GOP is now four-for-four in special congressional elections since Trump's victory despite media onslaught.

June 22, 2017

I suppose the natural reaction would be for me to offer up a nice reward to the first person who would bring me the head of one Johnny Depp. He's played Captain Jack Sparrow in the movies so he's well acquainted with a bounty. But that would just drag us on the Right down to the insane level that is America's present day Left. So, I'll just pray for him. And by the way, when did it become legal to threaten the president's life? It's been happening seemingly everywhere with seemingly zero consequences. Did I miss a memo? Perhaps the Secret Service needs to stop paying for South American hookers and get back to their job-no matter how shitty the pay. Yes, they are on Glassdoor too.

June 30, 2017 (On NYC Hospital Shooting)

Area Liberal breathlessly waiting on word of the race of the shooter to decide whether to embark on gun control rant or not.

July 11, 2017 (On All-Star Game Fact)

The MLB All-Star game 50 years ago in '67 in Anaheim was a great contest that lasted 15 innings and was won by the NL thanks to a homer by Tony Perez. A cool side note from that game was courtesy of The Mick. Mantle started that game, had an at-bat, and was lifted after. He then showered and left the ballpark, making his way to the airport for a flight back to Dallas. Once there, he pulled up to one of his favorite watering holes and, thanks to the lateness of the game, was able to watch the end of it on TV while having a cold one.

July 31, 2017 (On his Brief Tenure in Trump's White House))

Anthony Scaramucci business cards had just arrived hours ago too.

August 22, 2017 (On Dinner at an Old Chattanooga Favorite)

After hearing the loud, obnoxious conversation at the table next to me all night, here's hoping that ANTIFA does something about pharmaceutical sales managers.

September 15, 2017 (On London Terrorist Attack)

When I find out which Catholic group was behind today's attack in London, there's going to be hell to pay.

September 29, 2017

The NFL team that just threw a game to spite its' QB, Derek Carr, will be moving to Las Vegas in a few seasons. If they can be corrupted by one man standing for our National Anthem, how badly can they be corrupted when dealing in the moral cesspool that is Sin City?

October 7, 2017 (On Bonehead Girardi Mistake During Yankees Playoffs)

"I'm a stupid, stupid man. May God have mercy on my worthless soul for making the decision to procreate and pass my frass DNA on to my children. Mother of all that is pure and decent, what was I thinking?" (Joe Girardi, American League Division Series, Game 2, Post-Game Press Conference)

October 10, 2017

Why would anybody as handsome as Harvey Weinstein need to force women to have sex with him? Lmao! Alrighty, there's your laugh for the day.

October 26, 2017

Ladies and gentlemen, our long, national nightmare is over. Joe Girardi is out as Yankees manager! I will be hosting a champagne toast at Dantanna's at Lenox tonight at 8 p.m.

New York County DA Cyrus Vance ponders whether to seek indictment of Girardi on several counts of player mismanagement.

October 29, 2017 (On Astros Post-season)

Why does Craig Biggio always dress like he's a captain at Mar-A-Lago?

October 31, 2017

Folks, if there's something you want to do in life and are afraid you won't accomplish it, go for it! If Jimmy Kimmel can be successful, anybody can be successful, anybody.

October 31, 2017 (On Georgia Dome Explosion Announcement)

I want to go to this so I can yell out loud seconds after, "Has anyone seen Grandpa?"

2018

January 15, 2018

Sorry folks, but if your uber delicate sensibilities preclude you from maintaining sanity when you hear the possibility of someone using the term "shit hole countries" in private, then you've got larger issues to concern yourself with. Somewhere, somehow, something far less would push you over the edge at some point; -a missed highway exit, inadvertently drinking spoiled milk, an unscheduled Kardashian rerun. Yes, indeed, life has gotten to be too much for you.

January 26, 2018

I just ate my third Tide Pod of the day, and I still feel hungry.

January 28, 2018

Sorry folks, but the Pro Bowl and the way it's played lends itself to Hawaii weather, not rainy Orlando, where essentially, it's a two-hand touch game where you can't tackle out of fear of injury. Good luck, NFL. You've made so many wise decisions lately.

January 30, 2018

Sorry, folks, but I am predisposed at a meeting and my usual SOTU commentary will be preempted.

January 31, 2018

While I understand that today's tragic train crash was most likely caused by a stuck truck, does anyone else find it disturbing that as many as 200 members of Congress can travel together on something as historically unsafe as Amtrak?

February 4, 2018

Philadelphia completely burns to the ground in post-Super Bowl victory celebrations causing an estimated $2,136 in property damage.

Thousands feared alive in Philadelphia post-Super Bowl victory celebrations.

February 13, 2018

Feel good story of the day——When employees at a plant in Arkansas found out one of their coworkers had to walk 11 miles to work every day because he didn't have a car, they banded together and had him fired.

February 16, 2018

There have been 150 mass shootings (defined as four or more dead) in the United States since 1966. There have been 1077 people killed in these shootings in 52 years. On average, that's 20.7 people killed each year in the US in a mass shooting. 20.7, deaths, people.

Now, let's look at kidney disease, which kills 89,000 people a year in the US and is referred to by doctors as the "Rodney Dangerfield of diseases," in that it gets no respect. Trying to find kidney disease fundraisers is a very difficult task, akin to locating Amelia Earhart. Moreover, trying to raise awareness for this disease pales in comparison to any other top ten causes of death in the US.

Yet, we have a non-stop barrage of talking heads on television, housewives on social media, and unscrupulous journalists yelling hysterically about more gun control laws and mock-inducing moans about "Repealing and Replacing the 2nd Amendment" each time there is "mass shooting." Even though kidney disease kills 4,400 times as many people each year. I'm just using kidney disease as an example here. I could point to a host of other causes of death to illustrate my point. So why pick one over the other? Both are preventable and can strike without warning. But the anti-gun zealots will contend that "a mass shooting is a situation where a person intentionally inflicts death on another human. That's the difference."

OK, I'm glad they raised this point. If they care so much about one person inflicting death with a gun, then why not transfer that outrage to a city like Chicago? In 2016, 771 murders took place there and another 650 last year. The more intellectually honest and less politically correct among us know the answer to that question.

There are 13,000 homicides by a gun every year. About 20 of the victims die because of a mass shooting. Where's the sympathy for the other 12,980 victims? Are these deaths preferable because they took place over a longer period of time as opposed to four or more deaths in a quick, frenzied period?

Is alacrity the prime concern of those who choose to only speak following a mass shooting, even though mass shootings comprise a very small fraction of the overall shootings number? If this is a concern only when a mass shooting takes place and is used to restrict or ban semi-automatic weapons, would it surprise those arguing for stricter gun control that revolvers, shotguns and rifles were used 76 times in mass shootings in the US between 1982 and 2017? Are we having a debate about banning all guns now? Unlike the left in this country, we need to have an honest and intelligent discussion.

There are many reasons why these shootings occur. The FBI and local law enforcement knew about this monster (Nicholas Cruz) in Florida but appallingly didn't do anything about it (once again). Care for the mentally ill in this country is grossly inadequate. But the never-ending barrage of violence-filled images originating from the cesspool that is Hollywood and the video game industry is also to blame. The breakdown of the family structure and parental roles and not learning proper respect for life and property also factor in. While it's healthy to have a national debate about the maximum legal number of rounds a gun can fire, just focusing on gun control is sophomoric and will not solve the problem. And faux, selective outrage over certain types of deaths to further a political agenda will not help promote a healthy debate.

February 16, 2018

Mueller indictments are the biggest joke to date. You mean there are fake sites on Facebook? The hell are you saying? If you read the entire indictment, you will see these so-called conspirators also conspired to help Bernie Sanders. Hmmm.

February 16, 2018

Some sad news to pass on as AJ Benza has just confirmed the death of journalist Mike Walker. I just watched a great episode of *Autopsy: The Last Hours of...* focused on John Belushi, where he was interviewed prominently. It's ironic that as a journalist for the *National Enquirer,* Mike Walker's reporting was more fact-filled than that of most mainstream media outlets. Rest easy, Mike.

February 17, 2018

Banning Images of Chief Wahoo and letting Nicholas Cruz walk free: American Progressives, getting to the root cause of societal problems since 1913.

February 20, 2018

Can anyone pinpoint the exact moment when LeBron James turned into an asshole?

March 4, 2018 (On Oscar Ceremony)

Eva Marie Saint, Rita Moreno, Christopher Plummer? To bring the median age of tonight's Oscar's attendees down a tad, they should throw in appearances by Olivia de Havilland, Carol Channing, and Kirk Douglas.

March 14, 2018 (On Hillary's Speech)

Maybe the best way to spread the message of gender equality isn't by giving a speech accusing women of voting a certain way because their husbands do and then needing to be carried from said speech by two men. Just sayin'.

March 16, 2018 (On NCAA March Madness historic upset)

Absolute pandemonium. Congrats, UMBC! There's a first time for everything. Love watching history being made. Cinderella's dancing, baby!

"I had UMBC beating VA in my bracket." (Brian Williams)

April 3, 2018 (On Laura Ingraham/LeBron Controversy)

Kudos to Fox News for standing by Miss Ingraham. If you listen to the looney Left, you'd think NBA players and crisis response actors are a protected class.

April 4, 2018 (On ESPN's Worst Announcer)

Jessica Mendoza is the best baseball analyst in the game today! To suggest that she somehow got her job because she is a female and a minority is, well, honest and accurate.

April 13, 2018

All you need to know about James Comey is that his favorite Beatle is Pete Best.

April 15, 2018 (On James Comey Interview with *60 Minutes*)

So, Comey didn't think it was important to tell Trump that the dossier was financed by his political opponent? You can all stop watching the interview now, folks.

April 26, 2018

It will be a great day when the Left grants African Americans full emancipation by allowing them the freedom to voice an opinion that is diametrically opposed to their own.

April 30, 2018 (On 2018 WH Correspondents Dinner)

If Michelle Wolf is 32, then I'm 18.

May 1, 2018

You guys wanna' feel old? Andy Pettitte just became a grandfather.

May 4, 2018

Mexico Series. Dodgers-Padres. Because MLB loves to highlight the possibility of players being robbed/kidnapped at gunpoint by a cartel.

Mexico Series—Dodgers-Padres. I can almost hear Trump asking, "Why do we keep sending our players to these shithole countries?"

May 18, 2018

Well, folks, I'm officially an elderly Jewish man. I just went to Goldberg's, ordered the Matzo ball soup, and complained that it was too drafty in there. Looks like I'll be retiring to Ft. Lauderdale any day now.

July 1, 2018 (On the World Cup)

I'm pulling for Denmark, but I like the Croatian goalie. He reminds me of the guys at a kiosk in the Jersey City mall that I used to haggle with for cell phone deals back in the early 2000s.

Wow. The shot of the Danish watch party at the Aarhus waterfront makes the Vermont Republican Party HQ look like Don Cornelius' block party circa 1972.

July 1, 2018 (On LeBron Leaving Cleveland Again)

So, Cleveland, how exactly do you burn a jersey twice?

July 7, 2018 (On Russia at World Cup)

Make Glorious Goal for benefit of Mother Russia. Vlad is happy.

July 14, 2018

I never thought I would find myself in a position where I'm frantically driving around Buckhead to find an establishment that's open early so I can watch the battle for third place in the World Cup. Give it another year, and at this rate, I fully expect to be embracing Western-European-style Socialism. NOT!

July 29, 2018 (On Media's Obsession with Russia-gate)

Does anybody know what has been happening in the world for the past 20 months? American fake media has reported on only one made-up story. I'm sure there's other things out there.

August 2, 2018 (On Being Inspired by My Trip to the National Art Gallery in Bulgaria)

Enjoying some priceless works of art, or so I thought.

Here's the transcript of "To Catch a Patron."

Chris Hansen Narration:

The next man to enter the museum is 43-year-old George Hilway. Using the screen name ghilway75@gmail.com, he has been chatting with our online decoy, who works for Perverted Justice. Hilway believes she is a 15-year-old part-time employee of the National Art Gallery of Bulgaria. He asks about the price of admission, opening hours, and the kind of "exhibit" he can expect. The conversation turns very graphic when Hilway begins discussing Andrey Nikolov's works and asks if his classic 19th century nude paintings will be on display. Our decoy, ever so slyly, plays along.

Decoy: Maybe. LOLZ

GH: Does the museum have a favorite era for display? If so, what is it?

Decoy: IDK, I guess we're up for anything. 😊😊

GH: Your website says construction of main entrance is still ongoing. Will I need to enter through the rear?

Decoy: It's my first time, wouldn't that be painful? 😣😣

CH Narration: Our decoy then asks a very poignant question, one which will later be used in court to show intent on the part of our patron.

Decoy: Heyz, did you buy protection?

GH: I purchased that as part of the Expedia deal for insuring my trip for an additional $35.

Decoy: Sweet. Can't wait to meet you, boo.

GH: Umm, thank you. I've been looking forward to this excursion for a long time.

Decoy: Hurry up please. I'm so bored here all alone in this big museum. My boss doesn't get back for another week.

CH Narration: And with that, Hilway ends the chat and begins to make the long journey to Sofia, Bulgaria from Atlanta, Georgia in the dead of the night. He travels 5,455 miles in 14 hours. Hilway is what Perverted Justice calls a "fast mover."

Chris Hansen Interview: "It never ceases to amaze me how many men still come to the museum. Sofia was our 7th investigation at an exhibition in Europe. You'd think the word would be out by now, yet guys still show up. You see a guy like Hilway; 43-years-old, college-educated, good career, successful. And yet here he is, in a major art museum in Sofia, supposedly just on holiday. You just have to shake your head and wonder what he's thinking."

CH Narration: Hidden security camera footage shows Hilway paying admission and walking in the exhibit hall on the first floor. He looks around confused and mouths the words "Where's the Mario Zhekov collection?" He sees our decoy, asks her for a map and if there's an audio guide in English.

Decoy: Hey, you're even cuter than your Yelp pic. Did you remember to bring your Triple A card for the discount?

GH: Uh, thanks. Yes, I never travel without it, can't be too careful these days.

Decoy: Awesome. Hey, I just left some clothes in the dryer, I'll be right back, OK? Help yourself to some sweet tea.

Hilway looks confused. "Huh?"

CH Narration: Our decoy departs and that's when I make my entrance.

CH: Hi.

GH turns around looking stunned, "Hello. Um, are you the curator? I—"

CH: I'll get to that in a minute. Why don't you have a seat right over there and please, take your hands out of your fanny pack. What would you say you're doing here today?

GH: Uh, just wanted to check out the Exhibition of the EU Leaders Messages from Their Informal Dinner in Sofia on the Eve of the EU-Western Balkans Summit on May 17, 2018.

CH: You know, I... hear that a lot.

GH: Well, I'm sure you do.

CH: You act like it's no big deal.

GH: Is it?

CH: What's your name?

GH: My name is George. What's this all about?

CH: What are you really doing here today?

GH: Apart from checking out the museum, nothing.

CH: Nothing? See the problem with that, George, is I have a transcript of your online chat. So, you better start being truthful.

GH: Yeah, umm, pretty sure I am.

CH (reading from transcript). You thought it was OK to ask an intern if you could see the "Bust of a Young, Roman Woman?"

GH: Yeah. It's a famous 1927 sculpture from Kiril Todorov that I believe is housed here today.

CH: You go on to inquire about what other busts are on display. You ask her if there's a Groupon available. See, that right there is a felony.

GH: It is? Honestly, sir, I'm just here as an art lover.

CH: Sounds like you're a lover, all right. So, you just thought you would hop in your car at 2 a.m. and drive all the way from Atlanta, some 5,455 miles away to see if these classic works of arts were on display or not?

GH: No, I flew. And I'm just here on vacation and wanted to explore some culture.

CH: I'll bet you flew. So you just wanted to explore some culture? I hear that a lot as well.

GH: I'm sure you do. We're in a friggin' museum!

CH: What do you think would have happened if I weren't here today and you showed up?

GH: I'd be listening to a lecture on "Reconstruction as a Tragedy and Farce."

CH: I'll tell you what the farce is, this online chat here! There's something I should tell you. I'm Chris Hansen with Dateline NBC and we're doing a story about online art predators and patrons. Everything you've said and done since you've entered has been recorded.

GH: Damn I'd hope so. We're in a place with several billion-dollars' worth of artwork. Glad there's a security camera system in place, Chris.

CH: If there's anything else you'd like to tell us, we're more than happy to listen. But if not, you're obviously free to go.

GH: Uh, can I start the tour now?

CH: That's not up to me.

CH Narration. And with that, Hilway gathers up his fanny pack, museum map and audio guide and heads out past the gift shop and cafe and right into the hands of the Bulgarian National Police Service who are conducting a joint investigation along with Perverted Justice.

Bulgarian National Police Service: Get down. Get down on the ground!

CH: A subsequent search of Hilway's hotel room found a passport, a copy of *National Geographic's Traveler Bulgaria* and several print outs of Tripadvisor reviews of several more museums throughout the former Eastern Bloc.

Bulgarian National Police Service Commandant: If not caught, we do believe Hilway would be visiting several more exhibits throughout the EU.

CH Narration: And with that, *Dateline* wraps up another successful investigation into the weird and shocking world of men who instigate cultural experiences online. Up next, Lester Holt and a new angle with the Russia-Trump collusion thingy. Back after this.

August 17, 2018 (On Little League World Series)

Folks, it's that time of year again, when baseball fans all over the globe can stop wondering what the favorite movie is of the starting shortstop for Japan's Little League World Series team.

September 1, 2018 (On John McCain's Funeral)

Apparently, the seating chart at McCain's funeral is based on doppelgangers as Jay Leno is seated next to John Kerry.

New "Hubba Bubba" flavor. What is up with Billy chewing gum at funerals?

Can't wait to hear Trump's bashing of Meghan McCain: "Folks, did you watch the funeral? A disgrace! Yuge disgrace! Meghan McCain. Did you see her folks? How big has she gotten? I thought wearing black was supposed to have a slimming effect on you? Am I wrong? She's yuge. She makes Rosie look like John Podesta. Really, really yuge. In fact, my team has told me that the movie, *The Meg* is really, in fact, about her. Whaddya' think, folks? From now on, she's going to be 'Massive Meghan.' How about that, folks? Massive Meghan!"

September 17, 2018 (On Brett Kavanaugh Controversy)

Anybody heard from Judge Roy Moore's accuser recently? Hopefully, the GOP won't keep falling for this...but then again, it is the GOP, so anything is possible.

September 18, 2018

Just tell the Libs that Kavanaugh directed *Rosemary's Baby*.

October 6, 2018

Why is there replay in MLB? They still get half the calls wrong.

October 7, 2018

Is Soros required to offer COBRA for six months to Kavanaugh protestors?

One can only imagine how Judge Roy Moore must be feeling this week. The GOP fell for the Left's bullshit game with him. Glad they finally wised-up.

(On Ballsey Ford's Lack of Interest in More Investigations into Kavanaugh Allegations)

Jeez! I wonder why Ballsey Ford isn't interested in legally pursuing her bullshit allegations.

An extremely sad and disgusting unintended consequence of the deranged Left's synthetic sexual assault stories: "Attention all would-be rapists. Feel free to target, assault and rape women at will if you don't plan to run for office as a Republican or aspire to the highest court in the land as a Conservative. These are the only times when we pretend to care. Moreover, if you are actually guilty of such heinous crimes, please commit such acts after directing *Rosemary's Baby*, running for AG in Minnesota as a Democrat or challenging George Bush for the presidency in 1992. Then, we'll move the goalposts to "hasn't he suffered enough already," "he's a Muslim and untouchable" and "smear the accuser(s) because this is "what happens when you drag a dollar-bill through a trailer park." Signed, the Left.

October 8, 2018 (On Yankees in the Playoffs)

All rise for Aaron Judge Kavanaugh night in the Bronx. My man gonna' bat Squi in from second like it's a 1982 kegger.

October 25, 2018 (On Dems' False Bomb-a-thon)

Breaking News—Explosive-like devices reportedly found at the residences of Bigfoot, Mothman and the New Jersey Devil.

October 26, 2018 (On Cap One's Overzealous Fraud Protection)

At Capital One, we care about your account security. So, when any transaction comes up that we deem suspicious or unusual, our expert cyber security team goes into place immediately. First, we automatically decline any transaction over five dollars. Second, we notify the card holder via text, email, phone call, telegraph, and in-person visit by local US Marshall to verify transaction all while simultaneously deploying a SWAT team to the place of business where the transaction occurred and to the account holder's residence and workplace. Third, trading on the NYSE is halted for the day while the SEC conducts a prompt and thorough investigation. Fourth, if you do not receive a phone call from Secretary of Defense, James "Mad Dog" Mattis within the hour, you earn double cash back points on your next statement. At Capital One, we take fraud very seriously. We hope you do too.

October 26, 2018 (On Explosive Devices Sent to CNN/Time and Others)

Does anyone really believe that anything sent via US Mail could reach its' intended recipient?

November 6, 2018 (On Midterms)

If all these dead people can get to the polls for the Dems, then all our able-bodied alive folks should be able to get to them on our side. Red wave beats dead wave!

Is tonight the night CBS finally calls Ohio for Bush?

November 10, 2018

If Stacey Abrams doesn't know when it's time to stop eating, how could she possibly know when to concede?

November 16, 2018

Just remember, folks, it's not too late to vote in Georgia if you're a Democrat, so please get to the polls by the next court ruling.

Stacey Abrams finally concedes...that Oprah is skinnier than her. Blames it on "appetite suppression."

November 18, 2018

Stacey Abrams announces Super Bowl LI winner is New England Patriots over Atlanta Falcons. "While Atlanta will never officially concede anything to true Am3erican Patriots, at the end of the day, and after 21 months, the points just weren't there for us-even if this battle did go into overtime, which is where us Democrats usually do our dirtiest tricks."

"My third time conceding will be a charm." (Andrew Gillum)

December 2, 2018 (On the Passing of George H.W. Bush)

In other news, Dana Carvey's career will officially be over after next week.

December 3, 2018

I like 41, but I'm still all funeraled-out since seasons three and four of McCain. I DVR'd it but still not all caught up despite last Sunday's binge-watching.

USPS to suspend delivery in honor of George H.W. Bush. And this is different from every other day how?

December 5, 2018

I wanna know what you think, America! How much damage did Bob Dole do to his 2020 presidential bid with his lackluster performance yesterday at Bush's memorial? Call lines are open now.

2019

January 11, 2019

So just to recap, folks...

Federal Funding for studies on why lesbians tend to be overweight - Check.

Federal funding for a wall on our southern border - Sorry.

January 25, 2019 (On Family Kicked Off American Airlines Flight due to Odor)

How bad do you have to smell to get kicked off a flight to Detroit?

February 5, 2019 (SOTU)

The Designated Survivor is Rick Perry? WTF!

Hey Nancy, you don't have to read the speech. It's being delivered two feet in front of you.

Yes, choosing greatness is a partisan issue, apparently.

Pence's face says, "I am a man of decency," but his haircut says, "Run ten laps around the cones."

Happy that Pelosi and the woman Dems are showing their sartorial support for the Culinary Institute of America.

Adam Schiff is the kind of guy who probably reminded his grammar school-teachers when they forgot to assign homework.

Probably not the best move for the Dems, days after the Governor Northam scandal, to show up in white sheets.

Hours after deadline, junior SOTU speechwriter thinks, "America's crumbling infrastructure is always good for bi-partisan applause."

The Left is a ghoulish bunch. Exhibit A is their reaction to POTUS' words on late-term abortion.

Why is Stacey Abram's giving the response to the SOTU when she could be sassing Rerun, Dwayne, and Raj at Rob's Place?

February 8, 2019

It's OK to commit infanticide, no more air travel, 90 percent top tax bracket, police, and Tim Tebow are the bad guys, BLM and Colin Kaepernick are the good guys. As many have said before, "Liberalism is a mental disorder."

February 10, 2019

Chuck Norris is allowed to make the first move on Bumble.

February 27, 2019

You'd have to go to Bernie Madoff to find a character witness for Michael Cohen.

March 3, 2019 (On Transwomen Allowed to Compete in Olympics as Women)

The irony here is that after a long struggle by the Left to bring gender equality to all aspects of society, the introduction of trans-rights will destroy that and in essence, perpetually showcase the superiority of "men" in athletic endeavors.

March 8, 2019 (On Jussie Smollett)

Yet another incident of Black-on-myself crime.

April 14, 2019

Start tagging your Liberal friends here on FB and ask them if they will give shelter in their homes to illegals entering at our southern border. #Crickets

April 15, 2019

I like how we have to pretend we have no idea who started the fire at Notre Dame.

April 16, 2019

OK, I'll play along. I suppose Al-Qaeda was just "renovating" the World Trade Center on 9/11.

April 18, 2019

I'm keeping with the MSM theme of the week, was very happy to see my Yanks "renovate" the Boston Red Sox this series.

April 20, 2019 (On Kate Smith Controversy)

In a sane world, the Yankees would be investigating why every player on the team is on the IL, not racism claims from 80 years ago. #Distraction

July 24, 2019 (On Robert Mueller Testimony)

Elderly, hard-of-hearing, confused man takes day trip to Washington. I think it's so wonderful when our seniors get to leave the Home and see this great country!

This is not testimony; it's a commercial for Aricept.

Category: Putting Your Name on Document or Writings You Clearly Had No Association With. See Robert Mueller and Ben Affleck.

Lunch recess on Capitol Hill mostly Jerrold Nadler airplaning spoons of apple sauce into Mueller's mouth.

Apparently, knowing which US president appointed you US Attorney for Massachusetts, is outside of your "purview" as well.

July 24, 2019 (On Robert Mueller Testimony)

Today, I'm glad that Robert Mueller finally got to see and hear what was in the Mueller Report. Although it would have been better if each time a Congressperson read a part of it to his virgin ears, Rose and Valerie screamed "spoiler alert" from the gallery. Clearly, Mr. Mueller had limited involvement with this "report."

Alas, tonight, Mueller returns home and to, no doubt, his splendid collection of *Matlock* and *Murder, She Wrote* episodes he keeps in front of his VCR with the blinking 12:00. Back to private life, undoubtedly for good, for a man who has spent so many of his years serving the public. Decorated war hero? Yes. Competent US Attorney? Indeed. High-quality FBI Director? You bet. Pawn used by the unscrupulous Left in their fraudulent, hate-filled phony investigation into our president? Absolutely.

And this, apart from the many lives unnecessarily ruined by the Dems the last two years during this travesty of justice, is the real crime here. To have the last bullet-point of your otherwise fine resume be this distinction should be unconscionable. But then again, it's the American Left here and we've come to expect less….way less. To stoop so low that they used this man, clearly no longer of sound mind or possession of his faculties, as their poorly planned crux de gras in their faux election night 2016 back-up plan should have a lasting impact on the American psyche that will blemish Dems chances of electoral advancement for decades. To trade on his once-proud image as gravitas for this circus of insanity is very sad indeed. To trot him out, in his condition, to face all in a national audience and to be embarrassed to the utmost degree is melancholy at its most. We shall see the postmortem of this disturbing kabuki soon. The death knell for Dems? We shall see, but I'm not preparing to craft any obituaries anytime soon as it clearly seems the chasm between the peripheral of acceptable sanity and the Dems actions are at their widest point and growing. Wishing Mr. Mueller all the best.

As for the Dems, well, I'll leave you with a quote from Richard Nixon, "Always remember, others may hate you, but those that hate you don't win unless you hate them, and then you destroy yourself."

July 25, 2019

Harvard study finds that accidentally swallowing a bug healthiest thing 94 percent of Americans will eat this summer.

August 25, 2019

Because I value incredible baseball insight, I, like the rest of America, am looking forward to Jessica Mendoza broadcast the Yankees-Dodgers game tonight.

Friday night YES Telecast with A-Rod as guest commentator

Michael Kay: "Alex, how did you like hitting here (Dodger Stadium)?"

Alex Rodriguez: "It was great. A great park with a great batter's eye and a great atmosphere."

Sunday night ESPN with A-Rod

Alex Rodriguez: "I could not hit at Dodger Stadium. When I was here, I stunk. And it was difficult for me. You mentioned the batter's eye. For me it was difficult to see. You see how bright it is out there. There's just some fields you don't feel right."

Don't worry, America, as always, I'm paying attention on your behalf.

September 22, 2019

Jessica Mendoza is the greatest baseball broadcaster in history and anyone who disagrees likely has heard any other baseball game announced by any other broadcaster in history.

October 8, 2019 (On Minnesota Baseball Fans)

Major League Baseball would like to thank the 39,504 fans who squeezed into Target Field tonight instead of their regularly scheduled dialysis appointments.

The brooms are out at Target Field-but mostly for the Andrew Zimmern brisket sandwich/Fulton Beer vomit overflow. #Yankees

October 12, 2019

The next person that tells me Trump doesn't act "presidential" is going to get a verbal beatdown. What exactly does it mean to act presidential? Hmm? Is it smuggling women into the White House for extra-marital affairs? Is it beating your wife to a bloody pulp and then having to have Kissinger inform you all about it the next day because you were blackout drunk? Is it penetrating an intern with a cigar while eating a pizza? What exactly is it? So please, spare me your phony, elitist, hypocritical diatribes.

October 15, 2019 (On Dem Debate)

Why Does Marc Lacey sound like every female middle school librarian?

A 78-year-old having to reassure people that he is up to the task after his heart attack.

Anderson Cooper: "Congressperson Gabbard, in your estimate, what is the greatest threat facing America today?
Gabbard: "Overactive sebaceous glands."

October 20, 2019 (On Yankee Manager's Many Postseason Managing Gaffes)

At this point, I wouldn't be surprised if not only Boone isn't back at Yankee Stadium in 2020 but the 2003 American League Championship banner as well.

October 27, 2019 (On Al-Baghdadi's Death)

al-Baghdadi suicide: NFL immediately orders autopsy to test brain for CTE.

Please tune in to CNN tonight at 9 p.m. ET as we commemorate the life and work of Abu Bakr al-Baghdadi. Narrated by George Clooney, with clips and commentary from many on the Left. Have a favorite al-Baghdadi memory? Please send it to ac360@cnn.com.

Special programming note: There will be a moment of silence for al-Baghdadi tomorrow at 7 a.m. ET at the beginning of New Day with Allison Camerota and John Berman. CNNs regularly scheduled wall-to-wall nonstop reporting of phony Trump collusion stories promises to resume immediately thereafter.

October 28, 2019

A recent five-year comprehensive study by Harvard University concluded that nearly 50 percent of sign language interpreters standing next to politicians at news conferences are "just wiggling hands and making shit up." (AP)

November 19, 2019

Shifty Schiff really does look like someone capable of his alleged hushed crimes; a bug-eyed pedophile hiding in the bushes on every 1970's ABC afterschool special.

2020

January 13, 2020 (On the Houston Astros' Light Punishments)

So, what if there is no official removal of their ill-gotten 2017 World Series as now that banner is as tainted as the team itself and will always carry a Ford Frick-sized asterisk in the court of public opinion.

January 14, 2020 (On Dem Debate)

Did Biden just complain about only making $42,000 in 1973? That's $248,000 in today's dollars, Joe.

February 3, 2020

Prayers for Rush Limbaugh for a speedy recovery. God Bless you!

February 3, 2020

It's been said often but worth repeating, "Democrats are very generous... with other people's money." While each year we laugh at "Sleepy, Creepy, Cheapy" Joe Biden's charitable donations, or lack thereof, it seems he now has a contender for his miserliness. Minnesota Senator and fellow 2020 Dem. presidential hopeful, Amy Klobuchar gave a whopping $82 to her Alma Mater, Yale University in 2015. Charity starts at home, folks.

February 4, 2020 (On SOTU)

Nancy Pelosi arrives on Capitol Hill; her collagen will be arriving shortly.

Juan Williams' suit cries "political pundit," his hair screams "network know-it-all" and his mustache says, "how much Colombian Decaf did we sell last quarter?"

How much does it pain Pelosi to have to stand and applaud our president? More for physical reasons than political at this stage of her life I'm certain.

What is Nancy searching for in the speech? Hey, you can just look up and listen to it live!

Wow! Never ceases to amaze me how things like record lows in unemployment for minorities and disabled people suddenly becomes a partisan issue when there is a GOP president.

Criminal justice reform., tonight's first bi-partisan applause although Stitch had to look to Schumer to see if it was safe to stand and clap.

The attaché for the Venezuelan President is reminiscent of a Kanamit from the "To Serve Man" *Twilight Zone* episode.

Nadler to Jeffries to Schiff, these are the saddest of possible words.

Most of the bi-partisan applause on the Dem side tonight is coming from Senator Sinema of Arizona, who is also the first openly bisexual Senator in US history. Love how she spreads the love.

(On Dem Woman Outfits)

I think the fact they look like they're in white straitjackets says it all.

El Rushbo stealing the show.

Pelosi attempting to admonish her children is quite the spectacle. Symbolic of her disastrous tenure as Speaker of the House.

Ol' Stitch ripping up a copy of the speech like a drunken sore loser tearing up their losing ticket at the track.

Maybe the best SOTU of my lifetime. Kudos, Mr. President.

Maybe clothed in white sheets refusing to stand for African American children and record Black unemployment isn't the best optic for a party whose history includes the creation of the KKK, Jim Crowe laws, segregation and lynchings? Just sayin'.

While dumb, dimwit DNC-ers dither in Des Moines, Donald destroys dark, dastardly Dem delegation in DC.

To help raise their spirits after one of their more disastrous weeks in recent memory, I wonder how many Dem politicians will be appearing in blackface tonight in nearby Virginia?

February 5, 2020

Romney splits his vote on two impeachment charges. What a POS! However, DJT acquitted by a wide margin on both counts!

February 5, 2020 (On Reports that Pelosi Pre-ripped her SOTO Pages)

Not surprised since she also needs to have her food pre-chewed.

February 6, 2020

In a recent study, 95 percent of Democrats couldn't find Ukraine on a map. Eighty percent couldn't find the map.

February 7, 2020

Washington Post and CNN to fact check Trump's claim that Pelosi is "an old, mashed-up, drunken sack of shit."

February 9, 2020 (On the Oscars)

Sux that Pitt didn't heed Gervais' advice from the Golden Globes.

If anybody still doesn't think that the Left's push for Socialism isn't a push for Communism, just listen to Julia Reichert's speech at the Oscars tonight where she literally said, "Workers of the world unite."

No, there is nothing wrong with the volume on your TV; that was just Eminem in prime time.

Why is Joaquin still in Joker makeup for award acceptance? What? That's Renee Zellweger?

February 17, 2020

Happy Presidents' Day to all my Facebook friends who may or may not have served as commander-in-chief of the US armed forces.

(On Old Bloomberg Tapes Where He Says Minorities Don't Know How to Behave in Workplace)

Geez, is this jerk a train wreck of Camryn Manheim proportions or what? But, making a play for the racist vote as a Democrat candidate is probably the way to go since the party invented the KKK and passed Jim Crowe legislature. Midget Mayor Mike knows all these tapes are out there from the past 10 years.

February 17, 2020

A sample of Bloomberg campaign ad slogans now appearing around the country:

> "The buck stops at my segregated lunch counter."
>
> "All the way with the KKK."
>
> "In your heart, you know he's White."
>
> "Are you better off than you were four lynchings ago?"
>
> "Yes, we Klan."
>
> "Not too tanned, rested and ready."
>
> "It's the firehose, stupid."
>
> "Where's the sheet?"

February 19, 2020 (On Dem Debate)

Feeling left out that you're part of some demographic that Midget Mike has yet to offend? Tired of waiting for the Merciless Munchkin of Manhattan to assault your race, sex, or occupation? Then please tune into the Democrat debate tonight at 9 p.m. to be made fun of, put down or stereotyped by America's favorite hateful bigot billionaire. Mike promises he will get to you all.

Bloomberg to crowd in Vegas: "Never bet on black."

Just fact-checked Biden and he's right: Mike did call Obamacare a "disgrace." Don't worry, Mike, very few people have access to the Internet in 2020.

Bloomberg: "Jesus, it's not going like I thought it would! Ugh? Hey, who in the audience would like a million dollars? Yeah? Come on. Just raise your hands."

Mayor Pete seems disappointed upon learning what "Stop and Frisk" actually is.

How come Liberals always leave the biggest carbon footprint? Could it be that they really don't believe their bullshit?

(On Dems Piling on Bloomberg)

I thought midget bowling was outlawed?

Bowe/Holyfield? Cesar Chavez/Taylor? Nope!
Biden/ Sanders/ Klobuchar/ Warren/ Buttigieg/Bloomberg is now longest Vegas beatdown.

If these candidates really want to solve the world's energy crisis, they should figure out a way to capture the light reflection off Lester Holt's forehead.

The "Libtards" have literally degraded a political debate to the point where Biden has to brag about how poor he is.

"Hey, I've got six years of presidential eligibility left. You wanna' nominate me?" (95-year-old Jimmy Carter after watching tonight's debate)

February 25, 2020 (On Another Dem Debate)

When the debate to be leader of the free world quirky descends into a wine-throwing reality show fight between two morons about an NDA. Way to go, Libs.

When does the Smithsonian request Klobuchar's Purple Pieman debate outfit to be safely sequestered in perpetuity next to the Fonz's leather jacket and Archie Bunker's chair?

A group of soon-to-be Octogenarians telling you what they will accomplish for you in the future. Wow.

Sweaty Mayor Pete inquiring about this "boyfriend loophole thingy."

Listening to these insane devils yell uncontrollably makes my head hurt.

Jay Sebring had more control of the house on 10050 Cielo Drive than the "moderators" in tonight's "debate."

February 26, 2020

I can't believe that the Dems 2020 Campaign Slogan of "Promising to Round up all Black Men Ages 16-25" hasn't caught fire yet.

March 2, 2020

"It's great to be in a state where wearing blackface isn't frowned upon." (Mini-Mike in Virginia)

March 2, 2020

Biden enthusiastically accepts endorsements from Jack Welch and James Lipton.

March 3, 2020

Could Pocahontas be scalped in her home state? Bernie on a war path in Worcester? Don't count the delegates too soon and give MA to her, or she might have to be an Indian giver.

March 3, 2020

From a strategic standpoint, the DNC played this beautifully; getting Klobuchar (promises of VP) and Buttigieg (promises of amyl nitrite) to back out right before Super T, so the moderate vote will coalesce around Biden (which it is doing tonight), who they feel has the best chance against 45 in the general election. Donna Brazile, once again frustrated by reminders of her missteps as DNC chair four years ago, lost it on the air earlier today. And she is on the air tonight for live primary coverage. Any decent network would have, at a minimum, "temporarily suspended" her. So, if you're keeping score at home the past 24 hours, that's MSNBC-1 Moral Run, Fox News-0. And you have the Liberal Murdock offspring to thank.

March 3, 2020 (On Yet Another Biden gaffe)

Joe points to his sister as his wife. Dude, you already lost Utah.

March 5, 2020

Pocahontas is packing up the teepee.

March 19, 2020

You mean being an elderly, lifelong smoker with a serious pre-existing condition living in a state-run healthcare nation makes you fatally susceptible to a respiratory infection? The hell, you say.

March 20, 2020

Appreciate that the Murdock kids have turned Fox News into a giant episode of "Ask Dr. Oz Fan Mail Bag."

March 22, 2020

Irrational times we live in when the public is under lockdown, and the prisoners are being freed.

March 23, 2020

Looks like the despicable mainstream media, despite their bluster about all age groups being equally susceptible to this virus, has decided to exchange their regular reporters at the Coronavirus Task Force Briefing for interns. The average age of this group appears to be "Clearasil."

March 23, 2020

Joe Biden urges America to immediately step-up production of Aricept.

March 28, 2020

CNN and MSNBC to change name of running tally of "US Deaths from Coronavirus" to "Democratic Voters Added to Rolls for 2020."

March 30, 2020

Virginia governor orders state residents to stay in blackface until June 10, amid Coronavirus pandemic.

March 30, 2020

China announces it's best to keep one million Uyghurs in quarantine for another 12 years.

April 3, 2020

I'd like to now hear from the economic experts on this, the financial actuaries, the market gurus. Where are their graphs and charts as to the "no turn back point for our economy?" Where are their business death number models? How about trajectories of "financial deaths?" How many suicides can we expect when the media decides the pandemic is over and people have no jobs or businesses to return to? What will the crime rates be when unemployment hits 35 percent? What will be the long-term mental health and physical wellbeing of 337 million people? What will the final death toll be, in a decade when there is no American economy? Have they given this any consideration at all?

We've heard from the "medical experts." Good. But as DJT said about Fauci and I'm paraphrasing here, "if it was up to him, we would shut everything down for 18 months."

This, of course, is lunacy at its' highest order and not sustainable. The media will have you believe, like they and marketing pros are taught, that it can only be one choice or the other. Think of the "Coke or Pepsi" wars. There are literally dozens of different soft drink products on the market, but if you believe there are only two, it explodes the profits of that duo and helps to greatly mitigate the margins of the others.

So, the two choices they have before us now are: "It's lives or the economy." And as Comrade Cuomo added, "No one would pick the economy over lives." False equation, Sir. It truly is sad that so many think there are only two choices here. Why not a tempered approach? It's not that or this, we have infinite choices. By all means, continue social distancing, wash your hands frequently and use sanitizer as you see fit. Just keep in mind that overdoing it causes the body to not be able to fight bacteria, other germs, and infection, which is the opposite result of their intended use. Stop shaking hands and giving ridiculous "bro hugs" to someone you met 20 minutes ago.

Close the subway in NYC, the epicenter of this virus. Why this hasn't been done is mind-boggling. Quarantine the most susceptible of us, those with pre-existing conditions regardless of age and the elderly. Test early and test often. Quarantine the positives and quarantine those they've come into close contact with.

Do all these things, but keep the economy open, get people back to work, give people hope and paychecks, not government handouts and let's start slowly returning to "normal." My fear is that we have already done great damage to our nation's financial future. The shuttering of businesses and the seemingly endless stimulus bills will prove deadly, but it's not too late. We can change course That is my hope and I remain optimistic. You've heard from the medical experts and lil' ole me, now let's hear from the economists and put this all together with facts over fear. Bottom line: The cure for this pandemic cannot be worse than the virus.

April 5, 2020 (On Fauci)

At first, by telling us we have nothing to worry about, he invites the virus and pandemic here. Then, by neither doing a complete lockdown or full exposure so we develop "herd immunity", he keeps the virus alive and spreading. Having once created this mess, he tells us we can't go back to work, further keeping us in these dire straits and further continuing the destruction of our economy. Timeline of this is tantamount here. Quarters two and three will both be negative GDP growth -that's the literal definition of a recession. When would this be announced? Around the second to third week in October-right before the election. The Dems have been asking for a recession to get rid of Trump for two years (see Bill Maher's video on this). They may have found a way.

April 7, 2020

"If you don't have a mask, wear a scarf." We can't do that either, Dr. Birx, because you own all of them!

April 8, 2020

And just like that, America's decades long war against heart disease has been won with reports of heart attacks and strokes at record lows. Bravo, America! Bravo!

April 8, 2020

New York City wholly unprepared for alien invasion attack that killed all nine million residents within 15 seconds finds troubling Johns Hopkins Study published in the *New York Times.*

April 10, 2020 (On US Airstrikes Killing Al-Qaeda affiliated Terrorists in Somalia)

Or as CNN reported it: "Eleven Somalis die from COVID-19 within minutes of each other as virus spreads to African continent."

April 11, 2020

San Francisco Mayor Orders City's Homeless to Defecate At Least Six Feet From Each Other-Reuters

In what is the nation's first "shit- distancing" decree, San Francisco Mayor London Breed announced on Friday that to stop the spread of COVID-19, San Franciscans can either practice safe defecation of six foot from one another on city streets and parks or face a $500 fine.

"The model put in place by the Imperial College of London is clear. We can greatly 'flatten the curve' if proper 'shit-distancing' is practiced here," the mayor said.

Dr. Anthony Fauci, Director of The National Institute for Allergy and Infectious Disease and member of the White House Coronavirus Task Force, citing a recent research paper, agrees. "Da' evidence from da' double-blind, peer- reviewed study done by Johns Hopkins conducted over uh tree month period in Baltimore is very clear. Dis is no longer just anecdotal 'happy time' stories about proper crapping working. Dis is effective. We need dis here and I will be advising da' President to enact dis nationwide."

But not all are happy about the new law. Willie Dixon, a longtime San Francisco-area homeless man expressed his concerns. "I used to be able to drop a load whenever and wherever I wanted to, man....no matter how close I was to somebody-whether it was in Potrero Hill or The Mission or Golden Gate Park. Now I gots to be six feet away from others. That's not what this city was founded on; it was founded on peace, love and people getting together, man. I just feel like this is government overreach. Plain and simple."

Jerry "Blotto" Rogers, who calls an alley in the Tenderloin neighborhood home, echoed similar sentiments. "First, they tell us we have to use clean needles to shoot up. OK, fine, I swallowed my pride and went along with it. Now, I can't drop 'the Cosby kids off at the pool' to close to my ol' lady last who is doing the same thing? Man, Charlie warned us about this

50 years ago, man. They are coming for our civil liberties. I don't even recognize this city anymore."

The order goes into effect Sunday at midnight.

April 13, 2020

Let's just have all American businesses reopen tomorrow in all the Publix, ShopRite, Ralphs, Trader Joe's, Whole Foods, Walmart, Costco, liquor stores and gas station locations since you apparently can't contract COVID-19 there.

April 13, 2020

Looks like The White House Coronavirus Task Force Briefings are back on the air after a short hiatus. I heard they might replace the actor who plays the Dr. part though. He's horrible.

April 13, 2020 (On COVID-19 Mortalities)

If some lives aren't more important than others, then why are some deaths?

April 15, 2020

Chief Medical Examiner of New York City, Barbara Sampson, reclassifies deaths of Heath Ledger, John Lennon, Sid Vicious, Nancy Spungen, Paul Castellano, Malcolm X, Andy Warhol, Greta Garbo, Arthur Ashe, Leonard Bernstein, Jackie Kennedy Onassis, Ayn Rand, Rita Hayworth, Henny Youngman, Tennessee Williams, Allen Ginsberg, Richard Nixon, and Robert Fulton as "presumed COVID-19."

April 16, 2020 (On China's Coronavirus Actions)

Can someone please explain to me the difference between intentionally creating a bioweapon for use vs. letting infected patients travel freely internationally while you lockdown your county?

April 17, 2020

All these news people without makeup on remind me of the first Batman movie when the Joker poisons Gotham's beauty hygiene products.

April 19, 2020

We don't have a fair and balanced media in this nation; rather, a propaganda machine that Goebbels would even be ashamed of. Ninety percent of the White House press corps "reporters" are hateful, deranged sociopaths who are quietly rooting for serious upticks in COVID-19 deaths to use as a hammer against Trump in an election year. Think about that for a minute.

April 25, 2020 (On Chris Cuomo and Stephanopoulus Hypocrisy)

Gotta' love the scumbag elitists! Telling everyone else to #stayhomestaysafe while they're out and about. The worst of them, these two phonies who completely ignored social distancing and mask mandates, all while telling people who NEED and WANT to go back to work that they shouldn't. You ever notice that the people who have been telling all during this that they shouldn't be going back to work, are the very ones who will be fine financially no matter what happens? Having said that, I'll bet you five hundred Fredo's that Cuomo faked his diagnosis.

April 25, 2020

"Coronavirus can live on surfaces as long as up to the election," warn Dems and the media.

April 27, 2020

If you believed in and thought the falsehoods regarding Coronavirus were bad, just wait till the truths about our economic devastation.

April 28, 2020

Lakers give back PPP money, immediately furlough LeBron James.

May 3, 2020

They say hindsight is 2020; most of us can't wait for 2020 to be hindsight.

May 22, 2020 (On Biden's "You Ain't Black" Comment)

This crazy, demented bat has a history of making remarks like this against African Americans-so where are all the Libs who are up in arms over this?

Nowhere! So, the next time some lefty tells you they have a problem with Trump because they erroneously believe he's a racist or they mock outrage at the phony media narrative surrounding the Ahmaud Arbery case, just tell them they're full of feces.

May 26, 2020 (On George Floyd Protests)

And just like that, the Libs no longer cared about people not socially distancing in public.

June 1, 2020

Maybe the FBI and CIA should have been a bit more focused on ANTIFA the past few years as opposed to Trump, Michael Flynn, Paul Manafort and Roger Stone. Just sayin'.

June 1, 2020

The restaurants by me in Buckhead that decided to reopen the past month were all hit by the looters and vandals on Friday night while the ones that chose to stay closed were untouched. Not a coincidence.

June 9, 2020

Does anyone know if "Big Floyd: Dark Side of the Loon" funeral tour will be adding dates as I missed Minneapolis, North Carolina, and Houston?

June 10, 2020 (On Reports from Ex-coworker that Chauvin and Floyd Bumped Heads at Work)

So, if Chauvin murdered him over a personal beef, what does this do to the narrative that this was just another White cop who wanted to kill a Black man in another example of so-called racist police brutality? Even if that personal beef was racist in basis, it certainly would not be a legitimate, cerebral, rational, credible public indictment of police officers in general-unless another agenda was in play.

June 10, 2020

Jewish Comedian Larry Miller once opined that the best way to have acquired the financial fortune that was Middle East oil was for Israel to tell its' ignorant, terrorist neighbors decades ago, "Hey, let us help clean up that crap for ya." LOL. Are there not parallels that could be drawn today of certain "empowered" individual groups pretending to do good for the perceived less fortunate?

June 10, 2020 (On Cowardly Drew Brees Backtracking on Recent Kneeling Comments)

Drew Brees Apologizes for Winning Super Bowl XLIV: "It was honestly never my intention to disrespect or defeat the Indianapolis Colts. To all those Colt fans, please accept my heartfelt apologies and know that I will try to do better in the future."

June 16, 2020

Maybe Don Lemon was right when he said the biggest terrorist threat to America was "White men." It certainly seems that most of the ANTIFA bastards being arrested f¶or arson, vandalism and violence against law enforcement are Liberal, white males.

June 17, 2020

The fact that "defund the police" is being debated is insanity at a level not seen in decades.

June 17, 2020 (On Atlanta's "Blue Flu")

Silence on many police scanners here tonight. Conflicting reports on what zones called out sick/walked off. Some say most of all six in Fulton County. Our mentally incapacitated mayor is said to have called surrounding counties for assistance, and they all told her to go pound sand. Two weeks ago, the appropriately named Bottoms was considered as a running mate for the equally mentally deficient Biden. Tonight, she is running for her life.

June 18, 2020 (On Supremes Rule Against Trump Administration's Bid to End DACA)

So Chief Justice Roberts ruled that it was "arbitrary and capricious," sounding like Cosmo Kramer in doing so, and applying about the same level of intellect. So, in short, an illegal Executive Order by a Democrat can't be undone by a legal Executive Order from a Republican. Got it, Cosmo.

June 23, 2020 (On Bubba Wallace's Fake "Hate Crime")

More from "Fake Noose' CNN.

June 27, 2020

I find it laughable that some rather unenlightened people I have encountered the past five years would yell from the mountaintops that DJT is a fascist and that he planned on ruling with the iron fist of a dictator. He's led in no such way. Yet, these same individuals were/are dead silent when their governors and mayors, in the last three months, behave in the exact manner they feared Trump would.

June 28, 2020

For every action, there is an equal and opposite reaction-Newton's Third Law of Motion. Thus far, silent, and staid American Conservatives are disproving this.

June 29, 2020

Chicago Tribune Announces Plans to Publish Special Weekly Monday Supplemental Issue Dedicated Solely to City's Weekend Shootings.

July 15, 2020

And to those on the Left who are against reopening schools, please stop your prevarications that it's about the safety, health, and well-being of the children — the Left does nothing for altruistic reasons. Please man-up, woman-up, cis-up, nonbinary up, pan-up, trans-up and whatever-up and just admit to your deceitful, decrepit "hearts" that this is all about further injuring the economy in yet another unscrupulous attempt to hurt DJT in an election year. And if you're bereft the requisite mental wherewithal to connect the dots as to why keeping schools closed is a barrier to economic recovery, perhaps there's a good children's coloring book that will explain this to you that you can find at your local Barnes and Noble-you know, the few stores that the rioters and looters left untouched the last month or so.

July 24, 2020 (On Covington High Schooler's Massive Lawsuit Financial Gains)

McConnell signals next stimulus bill largely funded from Sandmann's lawsuit settlements.

July 24, 2020

Rob Manfred announces that all MLB teams to wear commemorative CCCP patches during "Turn Back the Clock" weekend.

July 25, 2020 (On Dr. Birx's Warnings that US is facing Three Virus Epicenters)

I'm sorry but I can't listen to someone who wears a scarf in 104-degree temperatures.

August 1, 2020

If I could sum up 2020 in one quote for all the flaccid sheeple out there, it would be this: "The urge to save humanity is almost always only a false-face for the urge to rule it." — H.L. Mencken

August 10, 2020

I always chuckle at these morons like Pelosi and her ilk who constantly warn the sheeple about Putin-even after all the BS phony Russian collusion delusions of the past four years. Is China not a billion times bigger threat than Russia? How many viruses do the Chicoms have to unleash? How much intellectual property do they have to steal? How much of our medical supply chain do they have to control? How much of our debt do they have to hold? How much of their currency do they have to manipulate? But no let's worry about Russia threatening to help nationalize another Moldavian vineyard or, hold on to your babushka, check passports at the made-up Transnistria border. Idiots.

September 20, 2020

The biggest mistake the American Right ever made was not engaging in cancel culture the way the Left consistently does. If you view politics as a game, and I surely do, it's akin to allowing your opponent a huge advantage that you agree to not partake in. Would you let your opposing Monopoly team start with a bigger treasure chest than you? Would you allow your gridiron opposition to score touchdowns while you could only kick field goals? Would you let your baseball diamond foes start their every offensive inning with the bases loaded while yours were empty? Of course not, that would be dumb. So why the handicap—no one is betting here, or are they? And if CC is not a useful tool, then why do Liberals consistently wield it? Because they know it works and that they can count on the spineless American CEO's, executives, and owners to kowtow to their bullshit movements such as BLM and ANTIFA.

September 29, 2020 (On Presidential Debate)

Someone check Biden's handkerchief for Wallace's lipstick.

There have been WWE Summer slam referees that have moderated more fairly. Still, Biden looks like a beaten, tired weakling. Trump's haranguing is working-if you can't handle a debate even when Chris Wallace is your tag team partner, you have no business being anywhere near 1600 Pennsylvania Avenue.

Wallace has spoken more than Biden tonight.

Just checked the schedule, apparently Trump and Wallace will debate twice more before the election.

October 20, 2020 (On Toobin Caught on Video Call Pleasuring Himself)

You ever notice how you never see Jeffrey Toobin and Pee Wee Herman in the same place at the same time?

October 22, 2020

Last minute, second VP debate added to slate with moderator Jeffey Toobin giving candidate Harris 25 minutes to rebut Pence in a "hopefully slow, soft, British accent with breathy pauses."

October 26, 2020 (On DJT Nobel Nominations)

Cuatro times nominated for Nobel Peace Prize—perhaps his street cred night be upped among the Librards if he had late-stage dementia and his kid was a crackhead? But hey, you can't please all the cretins, all the time.

October 27, 2020 (On "Can I Change My Vote" trending on Google)

You mean humans can actually change their minds (i.e., thoughts) as events unfold? There should not be early voting. It's called "Election Day" for a reason.

November 3, 2020 (Election Night)

Amazing how you can get 90 percent of the vote tally in a state in one hour and then you need six hours to get the last 10 percent. Dem Operatives searching for votes-won't work.

When has it ever happened where states stopped counting votes on election night?

Scared of giving DJT a victory at night and letting the rioters/looters have at it? If they announce these tomorrow in the daytime, states will have time to activate the National Guard? Perhaps less mayhem?

Damn you, Fox News. Calling VA and AZ way too early for Biden but won't call Trump for Ohio when he is up by eight with only 8 percent outstanding?

How can you not call Ohio, Stirewalt?

PMSNBC hasn't called Arizona, yet Faux News did hours ago—think about that for a minute. Wow, have times changed.

The ol' water line break in Atlanta story.

"Attention, Comrades. Please note that all ballots counted last are for Biden that were mail-ins from urban, deep blue areas. This is just how Pennsylvania, Wisconsin, Michigan, North Carolina, and Georgia all played out. There is nothing to see here. This is Pravda! Please continue to stay inside, wear your masks, and wait for your check from the Politburo. We will continue to update you with information we deem fit for you to consume from brothers Dorsey, Zuckerberg and Pichai. Obey!"

November 8, 2020

Would like to thank all the support from non-White voters for putting DJT on the brink of his second term when all the smoke clears. While it's disappointing that White male voters underperformed for Trump, his second term will be representative of them as well as all Americans. Trump got more support from non-White voters than any other GOP presidential candidate in 60 years. He received 35 percent of Latino voters, 59 percent of Native

Hawaiians, 52 percent of Native Americans, 52 percent of Native Alaskans and 18 percent of Black males - up from four percent support in 2012 for Romney.#KAG2020

December 12, 2020

Omnipresent headlines of local business owners who "lost it all during COVID-19 lockdowns/also voted for Biden" spur heavy trading on world's tiniest violins market.